THE STANDARD RESPONSE PROTOCOL
SRP
& THE STANDARD REUNIFICATION METHOD
SRM

HOLD

SECURE

LOCKDOWN

EVACUATE

SHELTER

REUNIFY

A General Guide from the Illinois Emergency Management Agency and Office of Homeland Security (IEMA-OHS) and the Illinois Fire Service Institute (IFSI) for Incorporating and Operating the Standard Response Protocol and the Standard Reunification Method within a K-12 Safety Plan.

2025 — The Standard Response Protocol and Standard Reunification Method - IEMA-OHS-IFSI

PEACE

It does not mean to be in a place where there is no noise, trouble, or hard work.

It means to be in the midst of those things and still be calm in your heart.

STANDARD RESPONSE PROTOCOL

SRP 2025 K-12 CHANGE HISTORY VERSION 4.2

AUTHOR/CONTRIBUTOR	VERSION	REVISION DATE	REVISION COMMENTARY
John-Michael Keyes	1.0	2009-03-02	Original content
Russ Deffner, John-Michael Keyes	2.0	2015-01-08	Version update
Tom Kelley (TxSSC)	2.1	2017-12-02	Content, edits, formal inclusion of the Standard Response Protocol Extended "Hold in your classroom" Texas School Safety Center version
John-Michael Keyes	2.2	2018-05-22	Content, edits. Colorado School District Self Insurance Pool version
John-Michael Keyes	3.0	2019-06-05	Incorporated "Hold in your classroom or area" into the Standard Response Protocol
John-Michael Keyes	4.0	2020-01-17	Replaced Lockout Action with Secure Action
Ellen Stoddard-Keyes	4.0	2020-06-23	Added new content and incorporated suggestions
I Love U Guys Foundation	4.1	2022-06-15	Additional guidance, detail and resources
I Love U Guys Foundation	4.2	2024-03-19	Additional guidance and detail

SRP 2025 K-12 CHANGE HISTORY _____ VERSION 1.0

AUTHOR/CONTRIBUTOR	VERSION	REVISION DATE	REVISION COMMENTARY
IEMA-OHS and IFSI	1.0	2025-06-12	Illinois-specific content added to SRP v4.2 and SRM V3

THE STANDARD RESPONSE PROTOCOL 2025 K12
A General Guide from the Illinois Emergency Management Agency and Office of Homeland Security (IEMA-OHS) and the Illinois Fire Service Institute (IFSI) for Incorporating and Operating The Standard Response Protocol and The Standard Reunification Method within a School Safety Plan.

ISBN: 978-1-951260-32-3

© Copyright 2025, All rights reserved. The I Love U Guys Foundation. SRP, The Standard Response Protocol, SRM, Standard Reunification Method, and I Love U Guys are Trademarks of The I Love U Guys Foundation and may be registered in certain jurisdictions.

FORWARD

The original concept of this program came from recognizing that most school safety plans focused on response to individual incidents. Since there is no way to predict every single type of incident, that method leaves gaps in response. It is fairly common, after a tragedy, to hear someone say "I didn't think that would happen here," so the assumption is that there was no response plan for it.

Many safety plans the Foundation looked at contained similar actions being used for the various incidents, but they were called different things. The Standard Response Protocol was developed with input from many safety practitioners and is action-based, defining each physical response. When the actions are practiced and understood, they can be used almost universally for any incident. This is a life skill that stretches far beyond school.

This book contains guidance on using the actions, as well as discussions and other considerations when using the Standard Response Protocol.

DEDICATION

On September 27th, 2006, a gunman entered Platte Canyon High School in Bailey, Colorado, held seven girls hostage and ultimately shot and killed Emily Keyes. During the time she was held hostage, Emily sent her parents text messages... "I love you guys" and "I love u guys. k?"

Emily's kindness, spirit, fierce joy, and the dignity and grace that followed this tragic event define the core of The "I Love U Guys" Foundation. This book is dedicated to Emily.

ACKNOWLEDGMENTS

The Keyes family is primarily grateful to responders A.J. DeAndrea (Arvada Police Dept., Ret.) and Mike Denuzzi (Jefferson County Sheriff's Office) for opening the door for discussion and communication in the aftermath of the tragedy, and to former investigative reporter Paula Woodward for making the introduction. (There's a story there…)

Thanks to Ted Zocco-Hochhalter for introducing us to emergency management for safer schools, to Katherine Zocco-Hochhalter for bringing humanity to the conversation, and to both for sharing their knowledge and friendship.

STAFF

The Foundation employees bring unique skills, curiosity and intelligence to the table.

BOARD OF DIRECTORS

Sometimes nonprofits have a variety of relationships with their Boards. We have always treasured ours for their dedication and wisdom. The Foundation strives for diversity and relevant professional skills in their board of directors.

AUTHORS AND CONTRIBUTORS

The Foundation is grateful to the people who have helped with the development of the programs. For contributions to content we are grateful to the following people:

Dr. David Benke (former teacher and former Board member) for Teacher Guidance;

Kevin Burd (Detective Lieutenant Ret., Priority of Life Training and Consulting) for content contribution and training expertise;

Russell Deffner (Advisor/Contractor/Volunteer) for Incident Command Guidance;

Pat Hamilton (Chief Operating Officer, Adams 12 Five Star School District, Ret.) for years of content contribution.

Tom Kelley (Texas School Safety Center, Ret.) for content contribution;

Ian Lopez (Director of Safety & Security, Cherry Creek Schools) for content contribution;

John McDonald (Jefferson County Public Schools, Ret.) for ongoing discussion and input on what's really going on in the world;

Joleen Reefe (City and County of Broomfield, Ret.) for the phrase, "Locks, Lights, Out of Sight";

Jaclyn Schildkraut PhD, (Executive Director, Regional Gun Violence Research Consortium, Rockefeller Institute of Government) for accuracy and research on drills and drill guidance;

Heidi Walts (Broomfield Police Department, Ret.) for being the best sister and sister-in-law to John-Michael and Ellen, and also giving excellent guidance when they needed it the most.

ADJUNCT INSTRUCTORS

Our talented pool of instructional providers conducts training around the country on a part time basis, bringing their expertise and knowledge to the table. And they bring back information about how we can improve the programs.

CONTACT INFORMATION

The "I Love U Guys" Foundation can be reached online at iloveuguys.org.

Email: srp@iloveuguys.org

Mail to:

The "I Love U Guys" Foundation
PO Box 489, Placitas, NM 87043

Answering service: 303.426.3100

"Tactics are intel driven."
What we plan is based on what we know.

"But the environment dictates tactics."
What we do is based on where we are.

- Deputy Chief A.J. DeAndrea
– Civilian Translation: John-Michael Keyes

TABLE OF CONTENTS

Introduction and Resources from The Illinois Emergency Management Agency and Office of Homeland Security, and the Illinois Fire Service Institute 8

The I Love U Guys Foundation Mission 10

Use of Materials in Illinois Schools 11

Terms of Use 11

Introduction 12

Overview of The Standard Response Protocol 13

Considerations, and How to Begin 14

Messaging and Communications 16

Hold. In your room or area. 18

    Sample Outward Messaging 19

Secure. Get Inside. Lock Outside Doors. 20

    Sample Outward Messaging 22

Lockdown. Locks, Lights, Out of Sight. 23

    Sample Outward Messaging 25

Evacuate. A location may be stated. 26

    Sample Outward Messaging 27

Police-Led Evacuation 28

Shelter. State the hazard and safety strategy. 29

    Sample Outward Messaging 30

Sequencing the Actions 31

Environment Dictates the Tactics 32

Drills vs. Functional and Full-Scale Exercises 33

SRP Lockdown Drill 34

Materials Available to Download 36

Frequently Asked Questions 40

The Standard Reunification Method 1

Dedication and Forward 3

The "I Love U Guys" Foundation Mission and About this Book 4

Terms of Use 5

Reunification 7

When and How to Initiate a Reunification 8

Introduction to the Incident Command System 10

Communication 12

Reunification Team Roles 13

On-Site Partial Reunification 14

On-Site Full Reunification 15

Off-Site Reunification Overview 16

Off-Site Reunification for a Non-Violent Event 18

Off-Site Reunification for a Violent Event 19

SRP Lifecycle with Reunification 22

Staging the School for Transport 24

Staging the Reunification Site 26

The Reunification Process in 6 easy steps 28

The Reunification Card 30

SRM Informational Handout for Parents 32

Signage 33

Frequently Asked Questions 34

INTRODUCTION FROM

ILLINOIS EMERGENCY MANAGEMENT AGENCY AND OFFICE OF HOMELAND SECURITY, AND THE ILLINOIS FIRE SERVICE INSTITUTE

The primary responsibility of IEMA-OHS is to better prepare the State of Illinois for natural, manmade or technological disasters, hazards or acts of terrorism. This initiative represents a collaborative partnership between the Illinois Emergency Management Agency and Office of Homeland Security (IEMA-OHS) and the Illinois Fire Service Institute (IFSI). Both agencies extend their sincere appreciation to the Illinois Homeland Security Advisory Council (IL-HSAC) for its ongoing support and strategic guidance.

- IEMA-OHS is charged with enhancing the State of Illinois' preparedness and response capabilities in the face of natural disasters, technological hazards, and acts of terrorism.
- As a national leader in life safety research, IFSI focuses on practical, action-oriented initiatives that directly benefit the daily work and safety of first responders.
- The IL-HSAC serves as an advisory body to the Governor, the Governor's Homeland Security Advisor, and IEMA-OHS, offering informed recommendations on homeland security laws, policies, protocols, and procedures.

MISSION STATEMENT

Illinois' Homeland Security mission is to build a safer, more resilient Illinois by prioritizing preparedness, prevention, and education. We empower communities with the knowledge and tools to identify and mitigate threats, while fostering collaboration across government and local partners to protect our residents and critical infrastructure.

VISION STATEMENT

We envision an Illinois where preparedness, education and prevention are the cornerstones of our Homeland Security efforts, and every resident is empowered to play an active role in building a safer, more prepared, and resilient state.

TOGETHER

The Illinois Emergency Management Agency and Office of Homeland Security, and the Illinois Fire Service Institute would like to acknowledge the Illinois Homeland Security Advisory Council for their support of this project and their on-going dedication to creating a safer Illinois.

THE STANDARD RESPSONSE PROTOCOL AND STANDARD REUNIFICATION METHOD IN ILLINOIS SCHOOLS

The Standard Response Protocol (SRP) provides a clear, shared language and set of actions for students, staff, and first responders during school-based emergencies. It is built around five simple actions: Hold, Secure, Lockdown, Evacuate, and Shelter. Each action is associated with specific directives and expectations, helping ensure everyone knows how to respond quickly and safely in any situation—from severe weather to active threats.

The Standard Reunification Method (SRM) supports safe and organized reunification of students with their families after an emergency. It outlines procedures for verification, accountability, and communication between schools, parents, and emergency personnel, reducing confusion and ensuring student safety during what can be a stressful time.

Together, SRP and SRM strengthen a school's emergency operations plan and enhance overall school safety by promoting consistency, preparedness, and community coordination.

ILLINOIS STATE RESOURCES

Illinois Emergency Management Agency and Office of Homeland Security
https://iemaohs.illinois.gov/

Email: OHS@illinois.gov

Illinois Homeland Security Advisory Council – Targeted Violence Prevention Committee
https://iemaohs.illinois.gov/hs/hsac/committees.html

Illinois Law Enforcement Training and Standards Board (ILETSB)
https://www.ptb.illinois.gov/

Illinois Fire Service Institute (IFSI)
https://www.fsi.illinois.edu/

STATE LEGISLATION

The School Safety Drill Act (105 ILCS 128/1)

Scan this for quick access to the page:

This Act states that the purpose is "to establish minimum requirements and standards for schools to follow when conducting school safety drills and reviewing school emergency and crisis response plans and to encourage schools and first responders to work together for the safety of children. Communities and schools may exceed these requirements and standards."

- One lockdown drill required within the first 90 days of the school year.
- Three fire evacuation and one bus evacuation are required. Language also states schools 'may' conduct additional evacuation drills to account for other evacuation incidents (ex. bomb threat).
- One shelter drill is required.

SCHOOL EMERGENCY AND CRISIS RESPONSE PLAN GUIDE

ISBE/OSFM All Hazard Preparedness Guide for Illinois Schools

If you have any questions, please contact HLS staff members at (217) 785-8779 or **hls@isbe.net**

Scan this for quick access to the site:

SAFE 2 HELP ILLINOIS

Safe2Help Illinois is an anonymous help line provided by Illinois Department of Human Services.

Safe2Help Illinois is available 24/7, and at no cost to all school districts in the state. In the absence of a trusted adult, students can use a free app, text/phone, or the website (**Safe2HelpIL.com**) to share school safety issues in a confidential environment.

Information obtained by Safe2Help Illinois will remain confidential to ensure student privacy and to protect the integrity of the program. This program is not intended to suspend, expel or punish students; rather, the goal is to encourage students to "Seek Help Before Harm."

MISSION
The I Love U Guys Foundation was created to restore and protect the joy of youth through educational programs and positive actions in collaboration with families, schools, communities, organizations, and government entities.

THE "I LOVE U GUYS" FOUNDATION
On September 27th, 2006 a gunman entered Platte Canyon High School in Bailey, Colorado, held seven girls hostage, and ultimately shot and killed Emily Keyes. During the time she was held hostage, Emily sent her parents text messages... "I love you guys" and "I love u guys. k?"

Emily's kindness, spirit, fierce joy, and the dignity and grace that followed this tragic event define the core of The "I Love U Guys" Foundation.

COMMITMENT
There are several things we are committed to. The most important thing we can do is offer our material at no cost to schools, districts, departments, agencies, and organizations. The reason we are able to continue to provide this service is due, in part, to the generosity of our donors and Mission Partners (see *Partner with Love* on the website). The "I Love U Guys" Foundation works very hard to keep our costs down as well as any costs associated with our printed materials. Donor and Mission Partner support allows us to stretch those dollars and services even more. Your gift, no matter the size, helps us achieve our mission. Your help makes a difference to the students, teachers, first responders, and the communities in which we live and work.

WARNINGS AND DISCLAIMER
Every effort has been made to make this book as complete and accurate as possible, but no warranty or fitness is implied. The information provided is on an "as is" basis. Please visit our website (**iloveuguys.org**) for the detailed information.

There are some links to resources in this book. In most PDFs they will be clickable, but the Foundation cannot guarantee that the actual source is still available at that site.

COPYRIGHTS AND TRADEMARKS
In order to protect the integrity and consistency of the Standard Response Protocol, The "I Love U Guys" Foundation exercises all protection under copyright and trademark. Use of this material is governed by the Terms of Use (details in the MOU and NOI documents) or a Commercial Licensing Agreement.

COMMERCIAL LICENSING
Incorporating the SRP into a commercial product, like software or publication, requires a licensing agreement. Please contact The "I Love U Guys" Foundation for more information and costs.

ABOUT SRP 2025
The I Love U Guys Foundation is committed to reviewing Standard Response Protocol materials every two years.

For SRP 2023, there was expanded guidance, the introduction of the "SRP Lockdown Drill," and new communications guidance. SRP 2025 builds on 2023 and offers further guidance on each the use of each action.

As you begin to implement and drill the protocol, keep in mind that environments are different. What that means is that we provide you with some tactics. Things we know. But your school, your agencies, and your environment, will ultimately dictate what you do.

THE "I LOVE U GUYS" FOUNDATION MOU
Some schools, districts, departments, and agencies may desire a formalized Memorandum of Understanding (MOU) with The "I Love U Guys" Foundation. For a current version of the MOU, please visit **iloveuguys.org**.

The purpose of an MOU is to define the responsibilities of each party and provide scope and clarity of expectations. It affirms the agreement of stated protocol by schools, districts, departments, and agencies. It also confirms the online availability of the Foundation's materials.

An additional benefit for the Foundation is in seeking funding. Some private grantors view the MOU as a demonstration of program effectiveness.

This can be emailed to **srp@iloveuguys.org**.

NOTICE OF INTENT
Another option is to formally notify the Foundation with a Notice of Intent (NOI). This is a notice that you are reviewing the materials but have not adopted them yet. This is also available on the website.

Minimally, schools, districts, departments, and agencies that are assessing the SRP and plan to incorporate the program into their safety plans and practices should email **srp@iloveuguys.org** and let The Foundation know.

USE OF MATERIALS IN ILLINOIS SCHOOLS

The Illinois Emergency Management Agency and Office of Homeland Security (IEMA-OHS) and the Illinois Fire Service Institute (IFSI) have contracted with The "I Love U Guys" Foundation for licensing of the SRP and SRM. This agreement allows the use of these materials by Illinois schools for crisis and emergency planning, prevention, response, and recovery at no additional cost and without further written obligation. However, previously documented copyright and trademark limitations still apply. Questions related to this agreement may be directed to Illinois Fire Service Institute Deputy Director JP. Moore at **jpmoore1@illinois.edu**

FAIR USE POLICY AND DMCA DISCLAIMER

These materials are for educational and informational purposes only and may contain copyrighted material the use of which has not always been specifically authorized by the copyright owner. In accord with our nonprofit mission, we are making such material available for the public good to restore and protect the joy of youth through educational programs and positive actions in collaboration with families, schools, communities, organizations and government entities.

The "I Love U Guys" Foundation IRS 501(c)3 est. 2006 asserts this constitutes a 'fair use' of any such copyrighted material as provided in Section 107 of the US Copyright Law. In accordance with Title 17 U.S.C. Section 107, these materials are distributed without profit to those who have expressed a prior interest in receiving the included information for criticism, comment, news reporting, teaching, scholarship, education and research.

If you wish to use copyrighted material from this site for purposes of your own that go beyond fair use, you must obtain permission from copyright owner.

If your copyrighted material appears in our materials and you disagree with our assessment that it constitutes 'fair use', contact us.

PRIVACY POLICY

When you agree to the Terms of Use by sending an MOU or NOI, your contact information will be entered into a database. You will receive notification when there are updates and/or new materials. You will have the opportunity to opt-in to receive periodic blog posts and newsletters via email.

Our Commitment to Program Users: We will not sell, share, or trade names, contact, or personal information with any other entity, nor send mailings to our donors on behalf of other organizations. This policy applies to all information received by The "I Love U Guys" Foundation, both online and off-line, as well as any electronic, written, or oral communications. Please see our website for the full Privacy text.

TERMS OF USE

Schools, districts, departments, agencies and organizations may use these materials, at no cost, under the following conditions:

1. Materials are not re-sold
2. Core actions and directives are not modified
    2.1 **Hold** - "In Your Room or Area."
    2.2 **Secure** - "Get Inside, Lock Outside Doors."
    2.3 **Lockdown** - "Locks, Lights, Out of Sight."
    2.4 **Evacuate** - A Location may be stated
    2.5 **Shelter** - State the Hazard and the Safety Strategy
3. The Notification of Intent (NOI) is used when the materials are being evaluated. A sample NOI can be downloaded from the website, and is provided to The "I Love U Guys" Foundation through one of the following:
    3.1 Complete the NOI and email it to **srp@iloveuguys.org**.
    3.2 Send an email to **srp@iloveuguys.org**.
4. The Memorandum of Understating (MOU) is used when it has been determined that the materials will be used. A sample MOU can be downloaded from **iloveuguys.org**, and is provided to The "I Love U Guys" Foundation by emailing it to **srp@iloveuguys.org**.
5. The following modifications to the materials are allowable:
    5.1 Localization of Evacuation events
    5.2 Localization of Shelter events
    5.3 Addition of organization logo

ONE DEMAND

The protocol also carries an obligation. Kids and teens are smart. An implicit part of the SRP is that authorities and school personnel tell students what's going on.

Certainly, temper it at the elementary school level, but middle schoolers and older need accurate information for the greatest survivability, and to minimize panic and assist recovery.

Note: Student training includes preparation for some alternative methods during a tactical response but reinforces deference to local law enforcement.

The Standard Response Protocol is a synthesis of common practices in use at a number of districts, departments and agencies. The evolution of SRP has included review, comment and suggestion from a number of practitioners. With each version, the SRP is subjected to tactical scrutiny by law enforcement agencies, and operational review and adoption by schools. Suggestions for modification can be made via email at **srp_rfc@iloveuguys.org**. Please include contact information, district, department or agency, including daytime phone.

STANDARD RESPONSE PROTOCOL

INTRODUCTION
This book outlines the Standard Response Protocol (SRP) and offers guidance on incorporating this protocol into a school safety plan for critical incident response within individual schools in a school district.

The intent of this document is to provide basic guidance with respect to local conditions and authorities. The only mandate presented is that districts, agencies and departments retain the "Terms of Art," which are actions, and "Directives" defined by this protocol.

The SRP is not a replacement for any school safety plan or program. It is simply a classroom response enhancement for critical incidents, designed to provide consistent, clear, shared language and actions among all students, staff and first responders.

As a standard, SRP is being adopted by emergency managers, law enforcement, school and district administrators, and emergency medical services across the country. Hundreds of agencies have evaluated it and recommended the SRP to thousands of schools across the US and Canada.

New materials and updates can be found online at iloveuguys.org.

A CRITICAL LOOK
Be prepared to look at existing plans with a critical eye, as often they can be described as a "Directive" of a certain "Term of Art." For example, conducting a fire drill is practicing a specific type of evacuation and the actions performed are similar in all evacuation scenarios. It makes sense to teach and train broader evacuation techniques while testing or practicing a more specific directive, like evacuating to the parking lot due to a fire.

TIME BARRIERS
Time barriers or measures taken beforehand to 'harden the structure' can be an invaluable asset to safety; not only for staff and students, but also visitors to a campus who expect a friendly and secure environment.

Time barriers are best described as a physical barrier that slows down the entry into, or movement through, a facility. Any additional delay allows trained persons to take further protective action and gives first responders more time to arrive.

An example of a time barrier is making the exterior doors of a building automatically lock, and could include installing a film on glass door panels to prevent them from shattering, thereby delaying an intruder's attempt to break into the premises.

THE POWER OF A LOCKED DOOR
Finally, the most powerful time barrier in an active assailant event is a locked classroom door. The Sandy Hook Advisory Commission Report* says this:

"The testimony and other evidence presented to the Commission reveals that there has never been an event in which an active shooter breached a locked classroom door."

In Foundation investigations of past school shootings where life was lost behind a locked classroom door, some edge cases were revealed. The perpetrator in the Red Lake, MN incident gained entry into the classroom through the side panel window next to the door. In the Platte Canyon hostage incident, the perpetrator was already in the room when Jeffco Regional SWAT explosively breached the classroom door. At Marjory Stoneman Douglas High School, shots were fired through glass panels in doors, but the perpetrator never entered any locked classrooms.

BEFORE YOU BEGIN
Districts and schools typically have a comprehensive safety program established and executed by a dedicated team of safety or security personnel. That same Safety Team should be responsible for incorporating the SRP into the safety plan. Including staff, students and a counselor or nurse on the Safety Team can greatly increase the buy-in and participation from all campus safety stakeholders.

> "SRP is not a replacement... it's an enhancement to your existing safety plans."

If it was not done during the development of the existing safety plan it is highly encouraged that, while incorporating the SRP, the safety team establish contact with local emergency services and law enforcement officials as they can help ensure safety plans will not conflict with existing local emergency services protocols.

FINAL REPORT OF THE SANDY HOOK ADVISORY COMMISSION
Presented to Governor Dannel P. Malloy State of Connecticut
March 6, 2015 - Document page 238 - Appendix A-I.1

HOLD SECURE LOCKDOWN EVACUATE SHELTER

THE STANDARD RESPONSE PROTOCOL OVERVIEW

A critical ingredient in the safe school recipe is the uniform classroom response to an incident at school. Weather events, fires, accidents, intruders and other threats to student safety are scenarios that are planned and trained for by school and district administration and staff.

Historically, schools have taken a scenario-based approach to respond to hazards and threats. It's not uncommon to find a stapled sheaf of papers or tabbed binder in a teacher's desk that describes a variety of things that might happen, and the specific response to each event.

SRP IS ACTION BASED

The Standard Response Protocol is based not on individual scenarios but on the response to any given scenario. Like the Incident Command System (ICS), SRP demands a specific vocabulary but also allows for great flexibility. The premise is simple: there are five specific actions that can be performed during an incident. When communicating these actions, each is followed by a "Directive." Execution of the action is performed by active participants, including students, staff, teachers and first responders.

- **Hold** is followed by "In your Room or Area. Clear the Halls" and is the protocol used when the hallways need to be kept clear of people.
- **Secure** is followed by "Get Inside, Lock Outside Doors" and is the protocol used to safeguard students and staff within the building.
- **Lockdown** is followed by "Locks, Lights, Out of Sight" and is the protocol used to secure individual rooms and keep students quiet and in place.
- **Evacuate** may be followed by a location, and is the protocol used to move students and staff from one location to a different location in or out of the building.
- **Shelter** is always followed by the hazard and a safety strategy and is the protocol for group and self-protection.

These specific actions can act as both a verb and a noun. If the action is Lockdown, it would be announced on public address as "Lockdown! Locks, Lights, Out of Sight." Communication to local responders would then be "We are in Lockdown."

ACTIONS

Each response has specific student and staff actions. The Evacuate action might be followed by a location: "Evacuate to the Bus Zone." Actions can be chained. For instance, "Evacuate to Hallway. Shelter for Earthquake. Drop, Cover, and Hold."

BENEFITS

The benefits of SRP become quickly apparent. By standardizing the vocabulary, all stakeholders can understand the response and status of the event. For students, this provides continuity of expectations and actions throughout their educational career. For teachers, this becomes a simpler process to train and drill. For first responders, the common vocabulary and protocols establish a greater predictability that persists through the duration of an incident. Parents can easily understand the practices and can reinforce the protocol. Additionally, this protocol enables rapid response determination when an unforeseen event occurs.

The protocol also allows for a more predictable series of actions as an event unfolds. An intruder event may start as a Lockdown, but as the intruder is isolated, first responders may direct students in parts of the school to "Evacuate to a different building," and later "Evacuate to the bus zone."

TACTICAL RESPONSES

SRP also acknowledges that some school incidents involve a tactical response from law enforcement, and suggests consultation with local law enforcement regarding expectations and actions.

SEQUENCING THE ACTIONS

As you read through the Action Sections, you'll see that the actions can be sequenced as situations change and information is gathered. See page 31 for examples of how this can, and has, been done.

STANDARD RESPONSE PROTOCOL

CONSIDERATIONS, AND HOW TO BEGIN
This section of the guidance gives references for building and progressing your Emergency Operations Plan. It defines conditions, actions, responsibilities and other aspects of preparing and incorporating the Standard Response Protocol into a school or district safety plan.

EMERGENCY OPERATIONS PLAN (EOP)
To create or review your EOP, a good resource is the Readiness and Emergency Management for Schools Technical Assistance Center.

Go to **rems.ed.gov**. Click the Tools button, and in the dropdown menu, choose K12 Emergency Management Virtual Toolkit.

PREREQUISITES: NIMS AND ICS
In order to coordinate the use of the SRP in district plans, it is highly recommended that key individuals within the district and those with a role in district/campus emergency operations, complete the following courses through FEMA.

1. IS 100.C: Introduction to the Incident Command System
2. IS-700.B: An Introduction to the National Incident Management System
3. IS 362.A: Multi Hazard Emergency Planning for Schools

These courses are available online at no cost at **http://training.fema.gov**. Anticipate one to three hours per course to successfully achieve certification. The courses are offered at no charge. Please note: The "I Love U Guys" Foundation is not affiliated with FEMA.

RESOURCES AND CREATING RELATIONSHIPS
Throughout this book, you'll see suggestions to contact local or regional responders. Whether it's law enforcement, emergency services, the fire department, or your county emergency manager, communication with these local resources is essential. Make sure to include the agency's dispatchers in any communication and relationship-building. In many cases, they will be your first point of contact in an emergency.

In most areas, schools are the largest population centers during a school day, so it makes sense to utilize the advice and services those agencies provide. Additionally, some county emergency managers are equipped to assist with your safety planning. Some school districts are able to engage with their regional Department of Homeland Security for training resources.

Take a look around your county and state to see what's available.

Also speak with your area hospital(s). If someone in the school or district suffers a severe injury, knowing how to communicate with them will be critical to advancing your outward communications to families and the community.

If you would like to speak with other schools or districts prior to utilizing the Standard Response Protocol, contact The "I Love U Guys" Foundation at **info@iloveuguys.org** and we may be able to connect you with a school or district near you that has a similar profile and/or similar challenges.

TALK TO THE FIRE MARSHAL
It's important to discuss classroom security options and modifications with local fire authorities, with gentle emphasis on life safety as well as fire safety. Some will allow a locked classroom door to be propped open during the school day, while some will not. Variances in local Fire Codes and applications will help determine the options for your schools.

DOORS, LOCKS AND STRESS
A consistent observation by first responders is that human beings have difficulty completing even routine tasks when they are under stress. The otherwise simple task of locking the classroom door may become extremely difficult for a teacher who has just heard a Lockdown order. Physiological responses may result in the loss of fine motor skills, which can impede an act as normal as inserting a key to lock a door. Therefore, consider installing locks which can be operated from the inside without a key.

STANDARD RESPONSE PROTOCOL

Keeping classroom doors locked during instruction has proven to be a time barrier. While this may create an inconvenience if students are late or need to re-enter the classroom for other reasons, it provides an essential layer of protection against intruders.

WHO STARTS?

For obvious reasons, a person in authority at the school or district level would have to approve the use of the SRP. While they may be the authority, however, it's usually a security person or someone from the safety team (Liaison) who actually initiates the process.

When an organization submits an MOU or NOI to The "I Love U Guys" Foundation, there's a space for the Authorized Liaison to enter their information, meaning they receive direct communication about updates and new materials. There can be multiple Liaisons.

Either way, the Liaison is the person who organizes and schedules internal training, puts up posters, and plans for outward communication. They may engage the district communication person to plan messages to educate parents and the community on the SRP.

TRAINING RESOURCES

SRP Training

While the SRP materials may be downloaded and implemented at no cost, the Foundation can provide on-site or online training for a cost, and has worked with a number of organizations in providing training workshops.

Find out more about training options at iloveuguys.org.

Do-It-Yourself Training

The "I Love U Guys" Foundation also provides a number of print, video, and presentation materials that can be downloaded.

It is recommended that refresher training be conducted for students and staff in schools at least once during the school year using the materials. This can be as easy as showing a 7-minute video. Check iloveuguys.org frequently for new and updated materials.

MEMORANDA OF UNDERSTANDING

Establishing a Memorandum of Understanding (MOU) and/or Mutual Aid Agreement (MAA) between responding agencies and local resources is critical. It is insufficient to rely on a conversation or handshake between entities who would respond to an incident or provide resources during an emergency.

Written agreements such as MOUs and MAAs are important to emergency operation plans and should be reviewed and updated regularly.

An SRP-focused Sample MOU between a School District and Law Enforcement/Fire/EMS was created in order to guide schools in creating effective MOUs with local first responders. Download it from the SRP section at iloveuguys.org.

WHAT ABOUT PARENTS AND GUARDIANS?

The Foundation provides informational SRP handouts for schools to send home or email to parents. These describe the SRP actions and directives, and also let parents know what they should expect to see and do during and after an incident.

While it's important to make sure parents understand this outward-facing part of your safety plan, finding the best method to deliver the information can be challenging. Here are some opportunities that schools can use to communicate the SRP to parents:

- Email a link to the parent handout from the school website twice a year. That can be accompanied by student lessons on SRP;
- Flyers at parent teacher conferences;
- A short training on Back to School night;
- School Accountability Committee safety procedure review.
- One district publishes a short magazine periodically to send to the parents with school information. They put in a 2-page spread on the SRP, along with articles about what's going on at the school.
- Highlight one SRP action per month, which emphasizes the all hazards nature of the program.
- Leverage a "captive audience" to review the SRP actions, such as before a concert, play, or athletic event.

MESSAGING
Email, Text, and Auto Dialer

COMMUNICATION

Every school's Emergency Operations Plan (EOP) should contain a section for communicating both internally and externally during a crisis situation.

In any type of incident, clear and well-planned communication is essential. Depending on the type of incident, you might have only minutes to prepare a statement and communicate it to the appropriate people.

Primarily, give the students and staff as much information as possible so they can make informed decisions about their actions. If little is known about the situation, tell them that.

Communication to parents and guardians is critical as well. It's likely that a number of them will show up at the school no matter what's going on, so letting them know what's happening and what to do is a must.

INCIDENT COMMAND

When your Safety Team is creating an EOP, they'll include some level of the Incident Command System (ICS), which is the hierarchy of authority and responsibilities. One role in ICS is the Public Information Officer (PIO) and this role can be used on a daily basis.

Having a Communication Team in your school and/or district is good practice in order to keep lines of communication ongoing for everyday events and activities.

Many school districts have a full-time Communication/PIO supervisor. Within a school, there is usually at least one person who manages the low-level event and activity communication along with their primary job.

High-level event information should be as clear, concise, and complete as possible. Create a policy for protocol and content for each communication channel to maintain consistency.

Document which people on the Communication Team are responsible for distributing messages through email, text, social media, and phone calls.

DIRECT COMMUNICATION

It is safe to assume that most schools/districts communicate regularly with the student families through email and text messaging.

In an emergency, add alternate methods for communication such as your student management system or automated calls. Doing so will alert the recipients that this is more important than daily communication.

Decide which methods of direct communication are the best fit for your community. This is reliant on your community's internet bandwidth, cell phone service, and other preferences. Whatever you choose needs to be reliable, fast, and reach a high percentage of the community

SOCIAL MEDIA CHANNELS

Most school day disruptions don't require any social media engagement, but if it is beneficial to alert the community of an incident, decide which channels are the best fit for your community. This is reliant on internet bandwidth, cell phone service and other preferences. Whatever you choose needs to be reliable, fast, and reach a high percentage of the community members. Document who on the Communication Team has access to update each channel.

The team should pre-script some basic messages that may be sent out, with blank spaces for details like time and date. Having these pre-approved and available will aid the team later if they're under stress or time constraints.

CONTACTS

After determining the best methods to use, decide who you will need to communicate with in each situation. Certainly staff and parents, but also students depending on the age group. Asking parents to keep their contact information updated is critical. Add responders, dispatchers, and media contacts as needed.

TIME

For certain incidents, there are only a few minutes to prepare. If Law Enforcement or Fire is involved, people will hear about an incident quickly. Reaching your stakeholders immediately with any type of message acknowledging the incident is essential. Have some basic message templates pre-approved and ready to use.

CONTENT

Not every situation needs immediate text messages and emails, so it's important to determine what is warranted and when. Less urgent situations—a school cancellation with ample notice, for example—might warrant an email, mass phone message and website update, whereas an unexpected early dismissal requires mass phone calls and text messages to ensure that information is received quickly.

An initial message can be as simple as stating that something has happened, and telling stakeholders where to find updates.

Include only the factual information you have; do not speculate. The recipients of your outgoing messages must be able to trust in the validity of the content.

Any situation that requires emergency communication for an incident will also require a follow-up.

If the school or district has a web page with information about what each SRP Action means and what the directives are, include a link to that page.

Plan on how you will be providing updates if those are needed, and include a link or reference to that site so recipients know where to look.

SAMPLE MESSAGING FOR EACH SRP ACTION

The following sections contain detailed instructions and considerations for each of the Standard Response Protocol Actions. Each section has sample messaging for that specific Action, and when and how it can be used.

CONSIDERATIONS

The district and school safety teams should develop guidelines outlining the types of communication to be used when Actions are called in different situations. Document this in the EOP.

Not all Actions will require an immediate communication response. For instance, if you anticipate a Hold or Secure taking no longer than 20 minutes, you may determine there is no need to send an immediate alert to parents and guardians. Do consider, however, that parents may receive communication directly from their child or from another parent. On matters related to safety, it's important to foster an environment where accurate and timely information is communicated to parents and other constituents.

PREPARATION

A tabletop exercise is a start; basically, it's a brainstorming session. Your Communication Team can talk through possible scenarios and formulate messaging accordingly. Think about what immediate information is necessary, how to follow up, and who they will need to speak with/follow to receive trusted updates.

The team should pre-script some basic messages for multiple scenarios that may be sent out, with blank spaces for details like time and date. Having these pre-approved and available will aid the team later if they're under stress or time constraints.

TWO MINDS

There are different messaging philosophies regarding how much information is too much information. In some events, a detailed description of the SRP Action and the steps taken by the school in response to the event are warranted. Guidance for this type of communication can be found under "Messaging to Parents" in the Hold, Secure, Lockdown, Evacuate, and Shelter sections.

For other events, a more generic message may provide enough information. The goal of the generic message is to inform the broader community that one of the SRP Actions was implemented but that no further action is required on their part. Think of it as a way to put parents, guardians, and others at ease.

Alternatively, the generic message can be used immediately following the protocol activation if details are unknown. In that case, use a statement that "more information will be sent out via (insert a link for them to click on)."

GENERIC STANDARD RESPONSE PROTOCOL MESSAGE TO PARENTS

Subject: Safety Notification - [School Name] Activated a Standard Response Protocol

Dear Parent or Guardian,

Today the Standard Response Protocol was activated at [School Name] due to [state the reason(s) that you used the action(s) of the Standard Response Protocol].

The safety and well-being of your child are our top priority. Learn more about the Standard Response Protocol at **iloveuguys.org**.

HOLD
In Your Room or Area. Clear the Halls.

HOLD
IN YOUR ROOM OR AREA.

There are situations that require students and staff to remain in their classrooms or stay out of access areas. For example, an altercation in the hallway may require keeping students out of the halls until it is resolved. A medical issue may require only one area to be cleared, with halls still open in case outside medical assistance is required.

There may be a need for students who are not in a classroom to proceed to an area where they can be supervised and remain safe.

PUBLIC ADDRESS

The public address for Hold is: "Hold in your room or area. Clear the Halls."

It is repeated twice each time the public address is performed. There may be a need to add directives for students who are not in a classroom, at lunch, or some other location where they should remain until the Hold is lifted.

"Hold in your room or area. Clear the Halls.
Hold in your room or area. Clear the Halls."

An example of a medical emergency message would be:

"Students and staff, please Hold in the cafeteria or your room. We're attending to a medical situation near the office."

PUBLIC ADDRESS - RELEASE

A Hold Action can be released by Public Address.

When it's been resolved:

"Students and staff, the Hold is released. All clear. Thank you for your assistance in making this Hold work smoothly."

INCIDENT COMMAND SYSTEM

The School Incident Command System should be initiated.

ACTIONS

Students and teachers are to remain in their classroom or area, even if there is a scheduled class change until the all-clear is announced.

Students and staff in common areas, like a cafeteria or a gym, may be asked to remain in those areas or move to adjoining areas like a locker room.

Students and staff outside of the building should remain outside unless the administration directs otherwise.

It is suggested that prior to closing the classroom door, teachers should sweep the hallway for nearby students. Additionally, teachers should take attendance, note the time, and conduct classroom activities as usual.

In a high school with an open campus policy, communicate as much detail as possible to students who are temporarily off-campus.

RESPONSIBILITY

Typically an administrator is responsible for initiating a Hold. However, anyone should be able to call for a Hold if they observe something happening that would require this action.

PREPARATION

Student, teacher, and administrator training.

Reinforce with students and staff that a Hold is "no drama." Classroom activities will continue while the incident is addressed. Administrators should make a plan for communicating with staff and/or parents after a Hold is cleared to provide pertinent information about the incident.

DRILLS

Hold should be drilled at least once a year, or as mandated by state requirements. The Illinois School Safety Drill Act does not require Hold drills.

CONTINGENCIES

Students are trained that if they are not in a classroom they may be asked to identify the nearest classroom and join that class for the duration of the Hold.

EXAMPLES OF HOLD CONDITIONS

The following are some examples of when a school might initiate a Hold:

- An altercation in a hallway;
- A medical issue that needs attention;
- Unfinished maintenance operation in a common area during class changes.

SAMPLE OUTWARD MESSAGING TO PARENTS

This is a guide for outward messaging after a Hold Action has been used in the school. Usually, it is sent after a Hold is cleared. However, if the Hold goes on for an extended period of time or it is happening close to release time, make sure to let the families know. Have a central digital platform that your public information team can easily update, and people can go to for information.

Variables in the message are bracketed and italicized.

CURRENT HOLD DURING THE SCHOOL DAY
Email
Subject Line: Safety Notification - Hold Currently Activated at *[School Name]*

Dear Parent or Guardian,

[School Name] has been placed in Hold due to *[state the reason for the Hold]*.

As a precaution, students and staff are asked to remain in their classrooms in order to keep the hallways empty. Classroom learning will continue throughout the Hold, but students will not be able to change classes.

The safety and well-being of your child is our top priority. We will continue to monitor the situation and update you further as soon as we have more information.

Watch for updates here *[link to the platform you'll be updating]*

What is a Hold Action? *

CURRENT HOLD AT THE END OF THE DAY
Email
Subject Line: Safety Notification - Hold Currently Activated at *[School Name]*

Dear Parent or Guardian,

[School Name] has been placed in Hold due to *[state the reason for the Hold]*.

As a precaution, students and staff are asked to remain in their classrooms in order to keep the hallways empty.

Student dismissal may be delayed for a short time until the situation has been resolved. You will be notified when students are dismissed. Thank you for your understanding.

The safety and well-being of your child is our top priority. We will continue to monitor the situation and update you further as soon as we have more information.

Watch for updates here *[link to the platform you'll be updating]*

What is a Hold Action? *

Text Message
[School Name] has been placed in Hold as a precaution. This situation may impact student dismissal. Please check your email for more information.

Phone Call
Parents, *[School Name]* has been placed in Hold due to *[state the reason for the Hold]*. As a precaution, we have placed the school in Hold to keep the halls empty. Student dismissal may be delayed for a short time. Please be patient. We will continue to monitor the situation and update you further as soon as we have more information.

NOTIFICATION THAT A HOLD OCCURRED DURING THE DAY
Email
Subject Line: Safety Notification - Hold Ended at *[School Name]*

Dear Parent or Guardian,

[School Name] was placed in Hold from *[start time]* to *[end time]* due to *[state the reason for the Hold]*.

As a precaution, students and staff were asked to remain in their classrooms in order to keep the hallways empty. Classroom learning continued throughout the Hold, and all school operations have returned to normal.

The safety and well-being of your child is our top priority. We will continue to keep you informed about important concerns at our school.

What is a Hold Action? *

---

* The Hold Action is used when the hallways in the school need to remain clear. Classroom learning will still take place as normal during a Hold, but students may not be able to change classes until after the Hold has been lifted.

Link to either your website or iloveuguys.org for them to learn more.

SECURE
Get Inside. Lock Outside Doors.

SECURE
GET INSIDE, LOCK OUTSIDE DOORS.
The Secure Action is called when there is a threat or hazard outside of the school building. Whether it's due to violence or criminal activity in the immediate neighborhood, or a dangerous animal in the playground, Secure uses the security of the physical facility to act as protection.

PUBLIC ADDRESS
The public address for Secure is: "Secure !
Get Inside. Lock outside doors" and is repeated twice each time the public address is performed.

"Secure! Get Inside, Lock outside doors.
 Secure! Get Inside, Lock outside doors."

"Students and staff, the school is currently in the Secure Action due to [cause] in the neighborhood. No one is allowed in or out of the building at this time. Stay inside and continue with your day."

PUBLIC ADDRESS - RELEASE
A Secure Action can be released by Public Address.

"The Secure is released. All Clear.
 The Secure is released. All Clear."

"Students and staff, the Secure is released. All clear.
Thank you for your assistance with making this Secure work smoothly."

ACTIONS
The Secure Action demands bringing people into a secure building and locking all outside access points.

Where possible, classroom activities would continue uninterrupted. Classes being held outside would return to the building and, if possible, continue inside the building.

There may be occasions when students expect to be able to leave the building - end of classes, job commitment, etc. Depending on the condition, this may have to be delayed until the area is safe.

During the training period, it should be emphasized to students as well as their parents that they may be inconvenienced by these directives, but their cooperation is important to ensure their safety.

ADDING A LIFECYCLE TO THE SECURE PROTOCOL
As a situation evolves there may be more information available to guide decision making. With the Secure Action, there is the option to transition from the initial response of "No one in or out" to some access control.

NO ONE IN OR OUT
The initial directive and practice during the Secure Action is to retain students and staff within the building and prevent entry into the building.

CONTROLLED RELEASE
An unresolved, but not directly evident, situation at the end of the school day may warrant a Controlled Release. During a Controlled Release, parents or guardians may be asked to pick up students rather than have them walk home. Buses may run as normal, but increased monitoring of the bus area should occur. There may be additional law enforcement presence.

MONITORED ENTRY
When there is a perceived threat but it's not immediate, entrances may be attended by security or law enforcement, and anyone entering the building is more closely monitored. Students and staff walking between buildings or going to the parking lot might be escorted with heightened awareness.

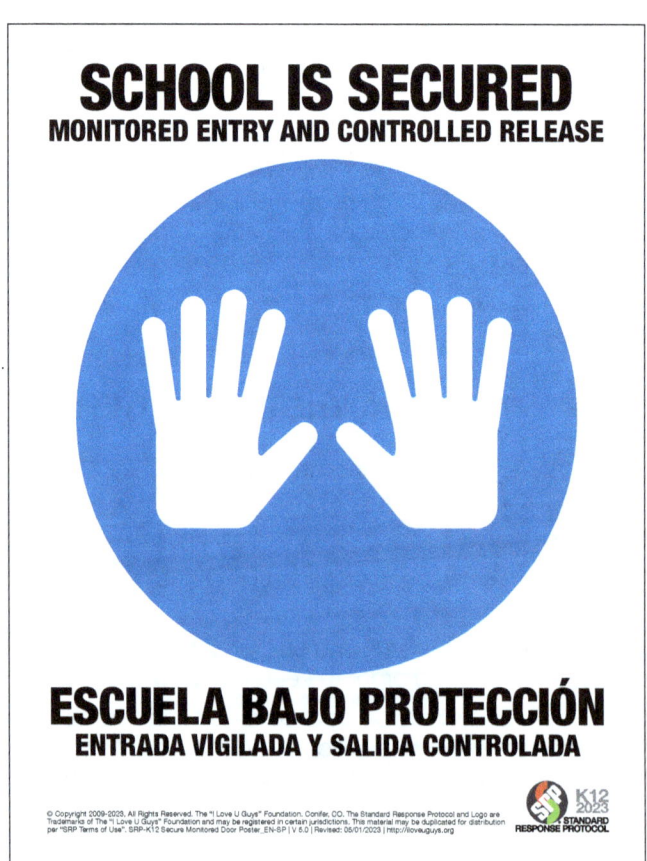

INCIDENT COMMAND SYSTEM
The School Incident Command System should be initiated.

RESPONSIBILITY
During a Secure Action, administration or staff may be required to lock exterior access points. Staff members assigned "Primary Responsibility" for a "Secure Zone" would follow the designated protocol during a drill as well. These areas may include doorways, windows, loading docks, and fire escape ladder access points. The assigned staff is designated as having "Secure Duty."

A person should also be assigned "Secondary Responsibility" for Secure Duty in the event the person with Primary Responsibility is absent or unable to perform the protocol.

Assign someone to attach the Secure posters outfacing to building entry doors, alerting potential visitors of the Secure condition.

REPORTED BY
Secure is typically reported by local emergency dispatch to the school office. The office staff then invokes the public address and informs the administration.

It may also be reported by students, staff or teachers if a threat is directly observed outside of the building.

PREPARATION
Identification of perimeter access points that must be locked in a Secure Action defines the perimeter. In the event a perimeter cannot be secured, identify areas within each building that can be secured.

Secure Zones - areas of a school or campus with exterior access points - should be established and protocols developed to ensure that those on "Secure Duty" attend to all areas in their zone.

Preparation includes identification of staff with Primary and Secondary responsibilities and the assignment of these duties.

DRILLS
Secure drills should be performed at least twice a year, or as mandated by state requirements. At least one should be performed while outdoor activities are in progress. The Illinois School Safety Drill Act does not require Secure drills.

CONTINGENCIES
There may be physical attributes to the campus that mandate special handling of a Secure Action. An example would be a campus where modular buildings are present. If the modular building cannot be secured, it may be best for students to Evacuate to the main building rather than going to Secure in the modular building. Listen for specific additional directives.

If the school is a distributed campus (multiple permanent buildings), they will have to consider what their perimeter is. In a perceived and indirect threat, they may decide that extra supervision for class changes between buildings is sufficient and appropriate.

If during a Secure Action, an additional hazard manifests (i.e.: fire, flood, hazmat), then additional directives will be given for the appropriate response.

EXAMPLES OF SECURE CONDITIONS
The following are some examples of when a school or emergency dispatch might call for a Secure Action:
- An unknown or unauthorized person on the grounds;
- Dangerous animal on or near the grounds;
- Criminal activity in the area;
- Planned police activity in the neighborhood.

SECURE AND HOLD
Sometimes people become confused about the difference between "Secure" and "Hold." During a Hold, the halls are cleared, students remain in their classrooms with their teachers and business continues as usual. If people are outside, they remain outside. During a Secure, people are brought inside, and all activities inside the school continue as usual but no one will move in or out of the building.

The main difference is that during a Secure, the halls are open and may be utilized by students and staff as needed. People inside the school may not notice any difference in their daily routines during a Secure.

Remember, the main difference between the two is that a Secure is enacted when a threat or hazard is outside of the school. A Hold is used when there is a need for the halls to remain empty, meaning the issue is inside the building. During both instances, classroom instruction should continue as normal.

SECURE
Get Inside. Lock Outside Doors.

SAMPLE OUTWARD MESSAGING TO PARENTS

This is a guide for outward messaging when a Secure Action is used in the school. Have a central digital platform that your public information team can easily update, and people can go to for information.

State in the message if the situation allows for Monitored Entry and Controlled Release. Variables are in the message are bracketed and italicized.

CURRENT SECURE ACTION DURING THE SCHOOL DAY
Email

Subject Line: Safety Notification - Secure Currently Activated at *[School Name]*

Dear Parent or Guardian,

[School Name] has been notified of *[state the activity occurring outside of the building]*. As a precaution, we have placed the school in Secure. During the Secure Action, all doors are locked and no one can leave or enter the building. *[Modify for monitored entry and controlled release]*

Watch for updates here *[link to the platform you'll be updating]*

What is the Secure Action? *

CURRENT SECURE ACTION AT THE END OF THE DAY
Email

Subject Line: Safety Notification - Secure Currently Activated at *[School Name]*

Dear Parent or Guardian,

[School Name] has been notified of *[state the activity occurring outside of the building]*. As a precaution, we have placed the school in Secure. During Secure, all doors are locked and no one can leave or enter the building. *[Modify for monitored entry and controlled release]*

Students may not be able to leave until the situation is resolved, and dismissal may be delayed for a short time. Please be patient.

Watch for updates here *[link to the platform you'll be updating]*

What is the Secure Action? *

Text Message

[School Name] is currently in Secure as a precaution. This situation has the potential to affect student dismissal. Please check your email for more information.

Phone Call

Parents, *[School Name]* has been notified of *[state the activity occurring outside of the building]*. As a precaution, we have placed the school in Secure.

Students may not be able to leave until the situation is resolved, and dismissal may be delayed for a short time. Please be patient.

Please check your email for more information.

NOTIFICATION THAT SCHOOL WAS IN SECURE ACTION
Email

Subject Line: Safety Notification - Secure Ended at *[School Name]*

Dear Parent or Guardian,

Today *[School Name]* was notified of *[state the activity occurring outside of the building]*. As a precaution, we placed the school in Secure. The Secure status lasted *[state the length of time in Secure]*. All school operations have now returned to normal.

What is the Secure Action? *

---

* The Secure Action is called when there is a threat or hazard outside of the school building. Secure uses the security of the physical facility to act as protection. During Secure, all students and staff are brought into the secure building and all exterior doors are locked. Classes are able to continue uninterrupted inside the building.

Link to either your website or **iloveuguys.org** for them to learn more.

LOCKDOWN
Locks, Lights, Out of Sight.

LOCKDOWN. LOCKS, LIGHTS, OUT OF SIGHT

Lockdown is called when there is a threat or hazard inside the school building. From parental custody disputes to intruders to an active assailant, Lockdown uses classroom and school security actions to protect students and staff from the threat.

PUBLIC ADDRESS

The public address for Lockdown is: "Lockdown! Locks, Lights, Out of Sight!" and is repeated twice each time the public address is performed.

"Lockdown! Locks, Lights, Out of Sight!
Lockdown! Locks, Lights, Out of Sight!"

ACTIONS

The Lockdown Action advises making rooms look unoccupied by locking individual classroom doors, offices, and other securable areas, moving occupants out of the line of sight of corridor windows, turning off lights, and having occupants maintain silence.

Most schools have implemented policies requiring all exterior doors be locked during the school day, consistent with current best practices. Therefore, the protocol advises leaving the exterior doors as is during a Lockdown Action. Be certain there's a plan for allowing local first responders to gain access during a Lockdown. The best option is to have the ability to lock and unlock doors remotely.

Training reinforces the practice of not opening the classroom door once in Lockdown. No indication of occupancy should be revealed until first responders open the door.

If the location of the threat is apparent and people do not have the option to get behind a door, it is appropriate to self-evacuate away from the threat.

INCIDENT COMMAND SYSTEM

The School Incident Command System should be initiated.

RESPONSIBILITY

The classroom teacher is responsible for implementing their classroom Lockdown. If it is safe to do so, the teacher should gather students into the classroom prior to locking the door. The teacher should lock all classroom access points and facilitate moving occupants out of sight.

REPORTED BY

When there is a life safety threat on campus, a Lockdown should be immediately initiated by any student or staff member. Initiating the Lockdown may happen through various methods, or a combination of methods, depending on the procedures and alert systems utilized by each school and district. Lockdown alerts may be made by word of mouth, phone, radio systems, intercom, panic buttons, or more advanced forms of technology. Plan the communication method in advance to set expectations for students and staff. Regardless of the method(s) of notification, the initiation of a Lockdown should be consistent, simple and swift, and include immediate notification of school administration and local law enforcement agencies.

PREPARATION

Identification of classroom access points that must be locked in the event of a Lockdown is essential preparation. These may include doorways, windows, loading docks, and fire escape ladder access points.

A "safe zone" should also be identified within the classroom that is out of sight of interior windows. Teachers and students should be trained to not open the classroom door, leaving a first responder, school safety team member, or school administrator to unlock it.

DRILLS

Lockdown drills should be performed at least twice a year, or as mandated by state requirements. The Illinois School Safety Drill Act requires one Law Enforcement Lockdown Drill to be held in the first 90 days of the school year.

A drill should always be announced as a drill.

For more information, see the "SRP Lockdown Drill" section of this book.

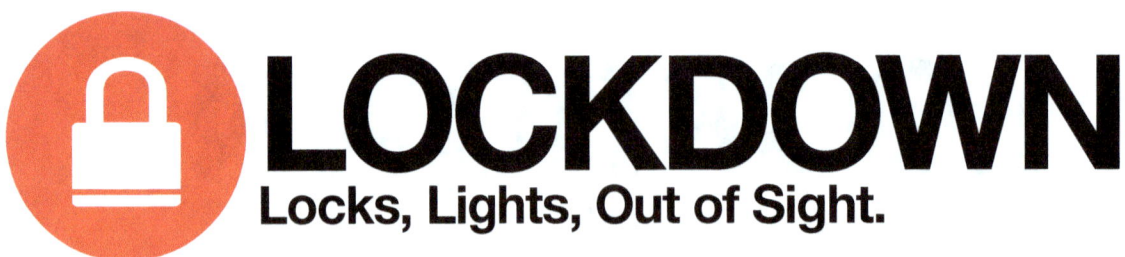

LOCKDOWN
Locks, Lights, Out of Sight.

CONTINGENCIES

Students and staff who are outside of classrooms when a Lockdown is announced should try to get into the closest available classroom, or room with a door that can be secured. In the event someone cannot get into a room before doors are locked, they should be instructed about other options. In this situation, students and staff should be trained to get out of sight, or even evacuate themselves away from the building or area. Students and staff should receive training on where to go if they self-evacuate so they can be safe and accounted for.

If during a Lockdown an additional hazard manifests inside the school such as a fire, flood, or hazmat incident, then situational decisions must be made. There should be discussions about reacting to a fire alarm if it is activated during a Lockdown. This may require following additional directives of the SRP.

EXAMPLES OF LOCKDOWN CONDITIONS

The following are a few examples of when a school or emergency dispatch might call for a Lockdown:

- Dangerous animal within a school building;
- Intruder;
- An angry or violent parent or student;
- Report of a weapon;
- Active assailant.

THE DURATION OF A LOCKDOWN

A question that occasionally arises is "How long does it take to release a Lockdown?" The answer is, "That depends, but probably longer than you want to hear."

The Foundation has heard accounts of a Lockdown lasting for hours. In one case - a weapon report - the school was in Lockdown for over three hours. In another - an active assailant in the building - it took about an hour after the issue was resolved for law enforcement to clear the classrooms.

RED CARD/GREEN CARD

Red Card/Green Cards should NOT be used for a Lockdown. Based on a number of tactical assessments, the overwhelming consensus is that this practice provides information to an intruder that there are potential targets in that room.

CELL PHONES DURING A LOCKDOWN

It is not uncommon for school administrators to ban cell phone use during a Lockdown. Parent instincts may be at odds with that ban. Often, one of the first things a parent will do when there is a crisis in the school is text or call their child.

In evaluating actual Lockdown events, the initial crisis may only take minutes. After the threat is mitigated, Law Enforcement typically clears the school one classroom at a time. This process may take significant time. During this time, both parents and students can reduce stress through text communication. This also provides a classroom management strategy. Selecting three or four students at a time, a teacher may ask students to text their parents with a message like this: "We're in Lockdown. I'm okay and I'll update you every 5 minutes." Certainly, if a threat is imminent, texting would be discouraged.

There is also an opportunity to ask the students to text their parents with crafted messages as an event unfolds. For example, "Pick me up at Lincoln Elementary in one hour. Bring your ID," might be recommended for student-parent reunification.

It may also be beneficial to have students turn off both Wi-Fi and cellular data services in order to free up bandwidth for first responders, while still allowing SMS text messaging.

EVACUATION

If an actual violent incident occurs, expect that the building will be evacuated by Law Enforcement since it has become a crime scene.

LOCKDOWN
Locks, Lights, Out of Sight.

MESSAGING TO PARENTS

This is a guide for outward messaging when a Lockdown Action is used in the school. Because a Lockdown is stressful for everyone, plan to send multiple messages. Have a central digital platform that your public information team can easily update, and people can go to for information.

If a Lockdown will be followed by an off-site evacuation, get that information out as quickly as possible. Include the information here, or in a separate communication thread.

Variables in the message are bracketed and italicized.

CURRENT LOCKDOWN
Email
Subject Line: Safety Notification - Lockdown Currently Activated at *[School Name]*

Dear Parent or Guardian,

[School Name] is currently in Lockdown due to *[state the facts you know about the situation]*.

The safety and well-being of your child is our top priority. We are actively responding to the situation and collaborating with emergency responders.

At this time, we ask that parents stay where they are and remain available to receive updates and instructions as needed.

Watch for updates here *[link to the platform you'll be updating]*

What is a Lockdown? *

Text Message
[School Name] is currently in Lockdown. Check your email or voicemail for more information. Please stay where you are and remain available at this time. Check here *[link to social media page/site]* for updates.

Phone Call
Parents, *[School Name]* is currently in Lockdown due to *[state the facts you know about the situation]*. At this time, we ask that parents stay where they are and remain available to receive updates and instructions as needed. Check our *[social media page/site]* for ongoing updates.

LIFTED LOCKDOWN
Email
Subject Line: Safety Notification - Lockdown Ended at *[School Name]*

Dear Parent or Guardian,

[School Name] was placed in Lockdown from *[start time of Lockdown]* to *[end time of Lockdown]* due to *[state the incident that occurred]*.

Thank you for your patience while we worked with first responders to respond to the situation.

The safety and well-being of your child is our top priority.

What is a Lockdown? *

Text Message
The Lockdown at *[School Name]* has been lifted. Please check your email or voicemail for more information.

Phone Call
Parents, the Lockdown at *[School Name]* has been lifted. The school was in Lockdown from *[state Lockdown start time]* to *[state Lockdown end time]* due to *[state the incident that occurred]*. Thank you for your patience while we worked with first responders to respond to the situation.

* Lockdown is called when there is a threat or hazard inside the school building. The Lockdown Action advises making rooms look unoccupied by locking individual classroom doors, offices, and other securable areas, moving occupants out of the line of sight of corridor windows, turning off lights, and having occupants maintain silence.

If students are unable to get behind a locked door, they are trained to self-evacuate.

If your child contacts you to let you know that they safely self-evacuated, please contact the district at [District Phone Number or Safety Hotline] to notify us your child is safe.

Link to either your website or **iloveuguys.org** for them to learn more.

EVACUATE
A location may be stated.

EVACUATE TO A LOCATION
Evacuate is called when there is a need to move people from one location to another for safety reasons.

An on-site evacuation is conducted usually because of a mechanical failure that would disrupt the school day, such as a power outage. If it can't be resolved quickly, the school may have to plan for early dismissal.

An off-site evacuation may be necessary when it's no longer safe to stay in the building such as a gas leak or bomb threat. In this case, people will be allowed to bring their personal items with them.

If there has been a violent event at the school, an off-site evacuation will almost always be necessary since the school will be deemed a crime scene. People may or may not be able to bring their personal items with them.

REUNIFICATION AFTER AN EVACUATION
When the students and staff are evacuated off-site, they may be walking to a different location or being transported to the location and there will be an organized reunification of students and parents/guardians at that site.

For in-depth information about conducting a Reunification, please refer to The Standard Reunification Method: iloveuguys.org.

PUBLIC ADDRESS
The public address for Evacuate is: "Evacuate! To a Location" and is repeated twice each time the public address is performed. For instance, "Evacuate! To the Flag Pole."

"Evacuate! To a location.
Evacuate! To a location."

ACTIONS
The Evacuate Action demands students and staff move in an orderly fashion to a safe area.

INCIDENT COMMAND SYSTEM
The School Incident Command System should be initiated.

RESPONSIBILITY
The classroom teacher or administrator is usually responsible for initiating an Evacuation. The directives or actions may vary for fire, bomb threat, or other emergencies. Other directions may be invoked during an evacuation, and students and staff should be prepared to follow specific instructions given by staff or first responders.

PREPARATION
Evacuation preparation involves the identification of facility evacuation routes, evacuation assembly points, and evacuation sites, as well as student, teacher, and administrator training.

An evacuation site may become the reunification site, so plan accordingly. Ideally, plan to have an off-site evacuation facility that's within walking distance, and another farther away from the school in case the hazard is in the immediate area. Have an MOU in place with each site to outline expectations and responsibilities in advance. A sample MOU for this can be downloaded from iloveuguys.org

An Evacuation plan must include having all supplies that people with disabilities may need such as medications, supplementary mobility devices and accessible routes for mobility-impaired people.

EVACUATION ASSEMBLY
The Evacuation Assembly refers to gathering at the Evacuation Assembly Point(s). Teachers are instructed to take attendance after arrival at the Evacuation Assembly Point(s).

Schools with large populations might plan on having multiple, predetermined assembly points to help manage crowds.

DRILLS
Evacuation drills should be performed at least twice a year or as mandated by state law. The Illinois School Safety Drill Act requires three fire evacuation and one bus evacuation drill per year. Schools 'may' conduct additional evacuation drills to account for other evacuation incidents (ex. bomb threat).

An Evacuation drill is very similar to a fire drill. Fire drills are often required regularly and constitute a valid Evacuation drill.

Drills are also a good opportunity to talk about and practice alternate exit routes to use in case a certain area is not safe to walk through.

CONTINGENCIES
Students are trained that if they are separated from their class during an Evacuation, then joining another group is acceptable. They should be instructed to identify themselves to the teacher in their group after arriving at the Evacuation Site.

RED CARD/GREEN CARD/MED CARD
After taking attendance, the Red/Green/Med Card system is employed for administrators or first responders to quickly visually identify the status of the teachers' classes. Teachers will hold up the Green card if they have all their students and are good to go. They hold up the Red card if they are missing students, have extra students or another problem, and use the Med card to indicate their need for some sort of medical attention.

See the Materials section for examples.

SAMPLE OUTWARD MESSAGING TO PARENTS

This is a guide for outward messaging when an Evacuation is necessary. Evacuations can be stressful because they are disruptive, whether they're on-site or off-site, so plan to send multiple messages. Have a central digital platform that your public information team can easily update, and people can go to for information.

Variables in the message are bracketed and italicized.

EVACUATION WITH A RETURN TO SCHOOL ANTICIPATED

Email
Subject Line: Safety Notification - [School Name] Has Been Evacuated

Dear Parent or Guardian,

[School Name] was Evacuated at [state evacuation time] due to [state reason for evacuation].

The safety and well-being of your child is our top priority. We are actively responding to the situation and collaborating with emergency responders.

The [state the reason for evacuation] is expected to be resolved with students returning to class. Dismissal will be at the regular time today. Watch for updates here [link to the platform you'll be updating]

What is the Evacuate Action? *

Text Message
[School Name] has been Evacuated due to [state reason for evacuation]. Please check your email and voicemail for details and information.

Phone Call
Parents, [School Name] has been Evacuated due to [state reason for evacuation]. Please check your email for details and information.

EVACUATION WITH EARLY DISMISSAL PLANNED

Email
Subject Line: Safety Notification - [School Name] Has Been Evacuated

Dear Parent or Guardian,

[School Name] was Evacuated at [state evacuation time] due to [state reason for evacuation]. Because of [reason], there will be an early dismissal at [state the time].

The safety and well-being of your child is our top priority. We are actively responding to the situation and collaborating with emergency responders. Watch for updates here [link to the platform you'll be updating].

What is the Evacuate Action? *

Text Message
[School Name] has been Evacuated due to [state reason for evacuation] and students will be dismissed early at [state the time]. Please check your email and voicemail for details.

Phone Call
Parents, [School Name] has been Evacuated due to [state reason for evacuation] and students will be dismissed early at [state the time]. Please check your email for details and information.

EVACUATION TO AN OFF-SITE LOCATION

Email
Subject Line: Safety Notification - [School Name] Has Been Evacuated

Dear Parent or Guardian,

[School Name] was Evacuated at [state evacuation time] due to [state reason for evacuation].

The safety and well-being of your child is our top priority. We are actively responding to the situation and collaborating with emergency responders.

At this time, we ask that parents stay where they are and remain available to receive updates and instructions as needed.

You will receive communications as soon as we have additional details and information on when and where to pick your child up. Please bring your ID and your patience when you are picking up your child.

Watch for updates here [link to the platform you'll be updating]

What is the Evacuate Action? *

Text Message
[School Name] has been Evacuated due to [state reason for evacuation] which renders the building unsafe at this time. Students can be picked up at [alternate location] after [time]. Please check your email and voicemail for details. Please bring your ID and your patience when you are picking up your child.

Phone Call
Parents, [School Name] was Evacuated at [state evacuation time] due to [state reason for evacuation]. At this time, we ask that parents stay where they are and remain available to receive updates and instructions as needed. We will update you with further communications as soon as we have additional details and information on when and where to pick your child up. Please check your email for details and information.

---

* Evacuate is called when there is a need to move people from one location to another. During an evacuation, students and staff are asked to move from one location to another in an orderly fashion.

Link to either your website or **iloveuguys.org** for them to learn more.

POLICE LED
Evacuation after a Lockdown

POLICE LED EVACUATION
In the rare situations where law enforcement is clearing classrooms and escorting students and staff out of the classroom and through the building after a Lockdown, it is important to have provided advance instruction on what to expect.

PUBLIC ADDRESS
There may or may not be any public address notifying students and staff that law enforcement is performing these actions.

ACTIONS
As officers enter the classroom, students and staff must keep their hands visible and empty. It is unlikely they will be able to bring backpacks, purses, or any personal items with them during a Police Led Evacuation. Students may be instructed to form a single file line and hold hands front and back, or students and staff may be asked to put their hands on their heads while evacuating.

WHAT TO EXPECT
Prepare students and staff that during a Police Led Evacuation, officers may be loud, direct, and commanding. Students and staff may also be searched both in the classroom and again after exiting the building.

EMOTIONAL RESPONSIBILITY
There is a conversation occurring with law enforcement regarding their role in post-event recovery. This is a growing concern and warrants conversations between schools, districts, and agencies about how to keep students safe, and reduce the trauma that might be associated with a Police Led Evacuation.

PREPARATION
Student, teacher, and administrator training.

In the event of a police-led evacuation, policies should be in place on how to give key access to law enforcement officers evacuating all rooms in the school building.

MEDIA MESSAGING
To the media/community after an event.

Example Situation: Violent Event

"On (date) at (time of day), (agency name) responded to (school name) in reference to (event type). Officers assisted with safely escorting students and staff out of the school and to the Evacuation and Reunification site where the (School District) was able to initiate the Reunification process."

DISPATCH MESSAGING
To responding officers during an event.

Example Situation: Police Led Evacuation

"(Dispatched Units) respond to (school name) to assist with Evacuation of students and staff. Assistance is needed to accompany individuals out of the school and to the Secure Assembly Area at (location). Respond to the Command Post for your assignment. (timestamp)"

LAW ENFORCEMENT MESSAGING
To responding officers during an event.

Example Situation: Gas Leak

(Police unit name) respond to (area near the school) to assist with evacuating students from (school name) because of a gas smell in the building. Meet with (supervisor) for further information to assist with Evacuation and Reunification.

LAW ENFORCEMENT GUIDANCE
Once the threat has been neutralized, it is recommended that first responders re-group and slowly move to the evacuation phase. Identify the location of the evacuation area or bus staging area prior to releasing classrooms. Take this time to discuss emotional responsibility when releasing classrooms. Begin releasing people from classrooms and offices to the designated area.

Law enforcement officers may also be needed to assist with directing traffic and ensuring the evacuation process is being done safely.

CONTINGENCIES
In an off-site evacuation to a reunification site, Incident Commanders should consider leaving students and staff in their rooms until transportation arrives. Your team can also discuss communicating to classrooms that the threat has been minimized enough that they may Hold in their classroom and wait for evacuation.

When it's time, each room can be cleared directly to the buses in order to minimize trauma.

It is recommended to avoid the scene of the incident when exiting. Transport directly to the Reunification Site.

TRANSPORTATION
During a police-led evacuation, transportation is going to be initiated. Have a policy in place for your transportation department or contracted transportation company so they are ready to respond in a timely manner with enough buses.

SHELTER
State the Hazard and Safety Strategy.

SHELTER
STATE THE HAZARD AND SAFETY STRATEGY
Shelter is called when specific protective actions are needed based on a threat or hazard. Training should include response to threats such as tornadoes, earthquakes, hazardous materials situations or other local threats.

PUBLIC ADDRESS
The public address for Shelter should include the hazard and the safety strategy. The public address is repeated twice each time the public address is performed.

"Shelter! For a hazard. Using safety strategy.

Shelter! For a hazard. Using safety strategy."

For a tornado, an example would be:

"Shelter for a tornado. Go to the tornado shelter.

Shelter for a tornado. Go to the tornado shelter."

After the danger has passed:

"Students and staff, the Shelter is released. All clear. Thank you for your assistance and patience during the Shelter."

HAZARDS MAY INCLUDE:
- Tornado;
- Severe weather;
- Wildfires;
- Flooding;
- Hazmat spill or release;
- Earthquake;
- Tsunami.

SAFETY STRATEGIES MAY INCLUDE:
- Evacuate to Shelter area;
- Seal the room;
- Drop, cover and hold;
- Get to high ground.

ACTIONS
Collaboration with local responders, the National Weather Service, and other local, regional and state resources will help in developing specific actions for your district response.

INCIDENT COMMAND SYSTEM
The School Incident Command System should be initiated.

RESPONSIBILITY
Sheltering requires that all students and staff follow response directives. Districts should have procedures for all foreseeable local hazards and threats which include provisions for those individuals with access and functional needs.

PREPARATION
Identification and marking of facility Shelter areas.

DRILLS
Shelter safety strategies should be drilled at least twice a year, or as mandated by the state. The Illinois School Safety Drill Act requires one Shelter drill per school year.

STATE THE HAZARD AND SAFETY STRATEGY
Using the Shelter Protocol and stating the hazard allows for an understanding of the threat and the associated protective actions. Most often, the Shelter Protocol is utilized for tornadoes and other severe weather, in which case it would include the Shelter location for students and staff, and what protective posture or action they should take.

Sheltering for a hazardous materials spill or release is very different. In the case of a hazmat situation, students and staff would be directed to close their windows, shut down their heating and air conditioning units and seal windows and doors to preserve the good inside air while restricting the entry of any contaminated outside air. Listening to specific directives is critical to successful emergency response.

PLAIN LANGUAGE
NIMS and ICS require the use of plain language. Codes and specific language that are not readily understood by the general public are no longer to be used. The SRP uses shared, plain, natural language between students, staff and first responders. If there are specific directives that need to be issued for a successful response in a school, those should be made clearly using plain language. There is nothing wrong with adding directives as to where to Shelter, or what protective actions should be used in the response.

CUSTOMIZATION
The classroom poster is sufficient for generic Shelter guidance. The Foundation recognizes that localized hazards may need to be added to the poster. For this reason, the Public Address poster is available in MS Word for customization: iloveuguys.org

SHELTER
State the Hazard and Safety Strategy

SAMPLE OUTWARD MESSAGING TO PARENTS

This is a guide for outward messaging when a Shelter Action is necessary. In a weather event, which is commonly the reason this is used, it's likely that families are also sheltering. They will want to know their children are in a safe situation. Have a central digital platform that your public information team can easily update, and people can go to for information.

Variables in the message are bracketed and italicized.

SHELTER (CURRENT)
Email
Subject Line: Safety Notification - Shelter Currently Activated at *[School Name]*

Dear Parent or Guardian,

[School Name] is currently Sheltering due to *[state reason for Shelter]*.

The safety and well-being of your child is our top priority. We are actively monitoring the situation.

Watch for updates here [link to the platform you'll be updating]

What is Shelter? *

Text Message
[School Name] is currently Sheltering due to *[state reason for Shelter]*. Please check your email and voicemail for more information.

Phone Call
Parents, *[School Name]* is currently Sheltering due to *[state reason for Shelter]*. The safety and well-being of your child is our top priority. Please check your email for more information. We are actively monitoring the situation and will send updates as necessary.

SHELTER (PAST)
Email
Subject Line: Safety Notification - Shelter Ended at *[School Name]*

Dear Parent or Guardian,

[School Name] used the Shelter Action from *[start time of Shelter]* to *[end time of Shelter]* due to *[state reason for Shelter]*. All school operations have now returned to normal.

The safety and well-being of your child is our top priority. We will continue to keep you informed about important concerns at our school.

Watch for updates here *[link to the platform you'll be updating]*

What is Shelter? *

Text Message
The Shelter at *[School Name]* has been lifted. All school operations have now returned to normal.

Please check your email and voicemail for more information.

Phone Call
[School Name] used the Shelter Action from *[start time of Shelter]* to *[end time of Shelter]* due to *[state reason for Shelter]*. All school operations have now returned to normal.

---

* Shelter is called when specific protective actions are needed based on a threat or hazard. Sheltering requires that all students and staff follow response directives based on the threat or hazard.

Link to either your website or **iloveuguys.org** for them to learn more.

SEQUENCING
the Actions

HOLD · SECURE · LOCKDOWN · EVACUATE · SHELTER

ENVIRONMENT DICTATES THE TACTICS
The five actions of the Standard Response Protocol can work together as situations evolve and information is gathered. Here are some examples of how this can, and has, been done.

HOAXES
False information may be reported to public safety about a threat inside the building. This situation may warrant a conversation with public safety agencies. If a threat is reported, but is suspicious, isolated or unverified, then a Hold action may be used in combination with a Secure action, instead of calling for a Lockdown.

This results in students being behind locked classroom doors and locking all outside access points. If the threat report proves false, it is easier to return to business as usual, than releasing the school from Lockdown.

HOLD ESCALATES TO LOCKDOWN
The school receives a vague or anonymous report, through social media, of a student carrying a weapon. There is neither an immediate confirmation of it nor a substantiated threat. School personnel need time to locate the student and send security/SRO to locate and engage the student in a very low-key way. They initiate the Hold Action during the search. Additional information and evidence may lead to a Lockdown because an imminent threat is detected.

HOLD TO EVACUATE
Utilize a Hold Action for a brief time during an unexpected fire alarm that is not accompanied by immediate signs of smoke or fire. This allows safety/security teams to scan for actual signs of fire, or other ambush type threats before Evacuating the building. An Evacuation would still occur per fire department requirements, but the tactical pause to gather information before evacuating allows for more situational awareness.

LOCKDOWN MISTAKE SHIFTS TO SECURE
The Police Department received reports from passers-by of a person with a rifle on the bike path adjacent to an elementary school. They called the school directly and directed them to put the school in Lockdown, which was incorrect but this can happen when there are many unknown factors. Officers and District Security Teams were on the scene within 2-5 minutes and a suspect was taken into custody within that time. Personnel on-site were able to quickly confirm the building wasn't breached.

The Lockdown was shifted to a Secure Action, with each classroom being released by school and security personnel. Releasing each classroom instead of using a public address is to retain continuity for releasing any Lockdown.

SECURE ESCALATES TO LOCKDOWN
Recently there was a shooting in a park adjacent to a high school. The school was immediately placed in Secure, however, several victims and witness students ran back inside before the doors could be secured. In this case, it was unknown exactly who entered the building. The Secure Action shifted to Lockdown as a precaution while officers searched the building. It was determined to be safe within about 30 minutes, but the Lockdown was not immediately lifted. Moving to Hold at that point may have been a better choice in order to manage the situation and maintain tactical control of the building while allowing some monitored movement inside.

ENVIRONMENT
Dictates the Tactics

WHERE YOU ARE DICTATES WHAT YOU DO

The SRP was designed as an all-hazards model for incident response. The protocol is easily modifiable for any location or environment. It is not necessary to list every possible scenario that may occur, as the protocol provides universal response actions. A school's action in response to a fire is an evacuation. To prepare for this evacuation drills are practiced, not fire drills. This is the same response that would occur due to a gas leak, or long-term power outage in winter conditions. By preparing for and practicing evacuation drills the school is prepared for any eventuality that may require the staff and students to leave the school location.

Your specific environment will dictate what additional plans or resources you may need. For example, a school in Alaska must think about warming locations for winter evacuations while a school in Arizona will need to think about cooling areas for a summer evacuation.

GLASS. LOTS OF GLASS

Glass is always one of the weakest points of building security. As more and more schools are built with the open concept, we are seeing walls of glass throughout buildings. While beneficial for increased light and a sense of openness, they provide little protection. If your school has interior glass walls or large interior windows we recommend you plan to purchase window film and some sort of shade system. The film will increase the strength of the glass and the shades will offer concealment.

Similar steps should be taken on the perimeter of buildings. Main entrances traditionally have large glass doors. Film is appropriate here as well. Be sure to inspect your school and note areas of potential weakness and address them appropriately.

DISTRIBUTED CAMPUS

Some school locations have a distributed campus with multiple buildings spread out over the property, similar to a college environment. The layout of a distributed campus brings unique challenges for school and district staff. Your jurisdictions will need to develop specific policies for each action. Additionally, it will be crucial for staff to be expertly trained on the process so they can use their judgment when needed. Nearly every action will have variations that may be necessary for a distributed environment.

Both Hold and Secure can be applied to the entire school property or only to specific buildings as appropriate. Whoever enacts the protocols will need to provide enough details for proper decisions to be made. If exact details are unknown then it is best to treat each building as an individual school and place the entire property into the protocol until more information is known.

During the Secure Action, there is some type of threat outside the school building. The action is for everyone to move inside, lock outside doors, and continue the day as usual. In a distributed campus more information about the threat is going to be needed.

If the threat is on school property, such as a dangerous animal roaming the grounds, then each building should go into Secure with students remaining where they are.

If the threat is off the property and a perimeter can be established then it may be appropriate for movement between buildings to occur but no one on or off the school property. An alternative approach could be to have security or law enforcement escort students and staff between buildings. The exact situation and your school's specific layout will determine your actions.

If the exact location of the threat is unknown, then it is better to err on the side of caution and keep everyone within their respective buildings.

A Hold will need to be handled similarly. If the reason for a Hold only affects a single building then it may be appropriate for only that building to go into the Hold protocol. However, you will need to make sure no students or staff are leaving other buildings and entering the Hold area.

TEMPORARY OR MODULAR BUILDINGS OR CLASSROOMS

Additional policy will be needed if your school has temporary or modular buildings. One option is to treat them in the same way as a distributed campus. Alternatively, if it is appropriate, and depending on the size of the school, students and staff from these areas can be brought into the main building.

DRILLS
vs. Functional and Full-Scale Exercises

DEFINITIONS
Here are some definitions and descriptions of drills and exercises. This is a compilation from various sources and includes the important points from each one. It includes information gained by experience with actual drills and exercises in schools and districts.

DRILLS VS. EXERCISES
Media coverage exploring issues with lockdown drills potentially causing trauma has resulted in the need for clarification. Much of the coverage attributed the word "Drill" to what was actually a "Drill Game or Functional Exercise."

School lockdown drills are not synonymous with functional exercises. Nor are they understood and practiced properly. According to FEMA (see Appendix A), exercises help build preparedness by allowing organizations to test and validate plans, determine strengths, and identify areas for improvement.

SCENARIO, OR NO SCENARIO
It is important to note that any type of exercise can be conducted with or without a scenario. The I Love U Guys Foundation recommends an all-hazards approach to exercise design and development, where the main goal is to practice or test a specific capability. For example, a functional exercise could be designed to practice interagency coordination in response to a large-scale power outage. The reason for the outage does not matter. At times a scenario can enhance the realism of an exercise but it is not needed.

The I Love U Guys Foundation uses this approach during reunification exercises and it is also recommended for Evacuation, Lockdown, Secure, and Hold drills.

DRILL
The primary objective of a drill is for participants to build muscle memory, and practice an action to use in various events or situations. A secondary objective is for the people who are administering the drill to validate procedures, clarify roles and identify operational process gaps.

Drills are for staff and students, and are educational opportunities to practice life safety skills. For example, an evacuation drill is conducted at schools worldwide regularly. A fire alarm goes off, students line up and head outside. Since there is no simulation of a threat or hazard, these cause less trauma.

Lockdown drills are similar. There is no simulated violence needed to conduct them. The only information needed is for the protocol to be enacted, "Lockdown, locks, lights, out of sight," and then students and staff perform the proper functions.

EXERCISE - TWO CATEGORIES
There are several types of exercises, which are divided into two categories. The categories are discussion-based exercises and operations-based exercises.

Discussion-based exercises are designed to introduce concepts to organizations. They allow individuals to become familiar with policies and procedures. Seminars, workshops, tabletops, and games are types of discussion-based exercises. Some of those will include talking about scenarios and regional hazards, and what sort of response might be required for those specific issues.

Operations-based exercises involve actual response actions and are used to practice or validate plans and policies. The learning objective is to test response, capacity, and resources across the system. Students are rarely asked to engage with these. An exercise can include a description or enactment of an incident, but doesn't have to.

Exercises are broader in scope than drills, and are designed to encourage people to think on their toes, work together, and apply lessons learned from drills.

Invite people from your community to participate as volunteers in an exercise, or to observe it. You will probably be introducing scenarios they have thought about, and this level of engagement can be useful.

In a Functional Exercise, participants perform their duties in a simulated environment. Functional exercises typically focus on specific team members and/or procedures and are often used to identify process gaps associated with multi-agency coordination, command and control.

The "I Love U Guys" Foundation's reunification exercises (Rex) are an example of a functional exercise. During these, participants test and practice the capabilities of the reunification team to properly reunite students with the appropriate parent or guardian. The exercise starts with notification that students were evacuated from the school and are already at the reunification site.

A Full-Scale exercise is similar in execution to a Functional exercise and is as close to the real thing as possible. It can include employees from multiple functions, community first responders, local businesses, and regulatory agencies. This type of exercise should utilize, to the extent possible, the actual systems and equipment that would be dispatched during a real incident. From a duration standpoint, full-scale exercises often take place over the course of an entire business day.

SRP
Lockdown Drill

SRP EVOLUTION
In developing the Standard Response Protocol, The "I Love U Guys" Foundation took the following approach:
- Identify the hazard;
- Develop response;
- Train;
- Practice;
- Drill;
- Exercise.

PROBLEM IDENTIFICATION
The first priority of the SRP was to introduce common, plain-language responses to various events. An assessment of various school responses in 2009 revealed there was no common language between students, staff, parents, media, and first responders. The core areas examined were:
- Something happening outside the school;
- Something is happening inside of the school;
- How to get out of the school;
- Natural or man-made hazards;
- Keeping the halls clear.

DEVELOP RESPONSE
Given those conditions, the Standard Response Protocol was developed, piloted and released.

TRAIN
The next step in the process is providing training to students and staff on each of the response protocols, which can be done with the downloadable materials.

PRACTICE
Once training has been delivered, practice is recommended prior to any drill. This may initially involve a discussion between staff and students to:
- Find various exit routes in advance of an Evacuation drill;
- Discuss ways to protect oneself from various weather hazards prior to a Shelter drill;
- Identify Safe Zones within a classroom and practice moving students to those zones prior to a Lockdown drill;
- Talk about situations that may require a Secure or Hold action.

COMMUNICATING ABOUT DRILLS
Prior to conducting any drills, schools are advised to send concise communication to parents and guardians about the nature and objectives of, and reason for, the drill. This can be done with an email or letter or both. It is not necessary to state the exact day or time of certain drills.

If parents feel their student(s) will be upset by certain drills, invite them to attend, or give them a chance to opt their family out of the drill. If possible, arrange to have an opt-out student stay on school grounds, but not participate, in order to minimize disruption to the school day.

LOCKDOWN DRILL GUIDANCE
A critical aspect of implementing the SRP with fidelity is the Lockdown Drill. Successful drills provide participants with the "muscle memory" should an actual Lockdown occur. Drills also reveal deficiencies that may exist in either procedures, training or personnel.

Understand that a Lockdown drill is for practicing an action, not an event. An actual Lockdown can occur due to a variety of threatening situations which may present an immediate and ongoing danger to the safety of students, staff and visitors within a building.

PREPARATION
Prior to drilling, students, staff and administration should review the SRP Training Presentation, which is available at iloveuguys.org. Administration should also verify with law enforcement their use of the SRP in the school or district.

Teachers should take time with students to identify and occupy a "Safe Zone" in the classroom where they cannot be seen through any corridor windows. If visibility in a classroom is problematic, window coverings or alternative locations should be identified. Speak with local law enforcement about their preference for using window coverings.

Additionally, the following instructions should be delivered to students.
- Locate yourself at a point in the classroom where you can no longer see out the corridor window.
- Maintain silence. No cell phone calls.
- Discuss the cell phone policy based on Lockdown guidance on page 24.

PARTNERSHIPS
School-level drills should have district support. There may also be district resources available to assist in conducting the drill. Another key partnership is with local law enforcement. Local patrol, community resource officers or school resource officers should be part of the drill process.

THE EMERGENCY RESPONSE TEAM

Some schools have a pre-identified Building/School Emergency Response Team. These teams are effective for responding to any type of incident.

It is a noted best practice for administration to survey the staff population for prior emergency response, military or law enforcement experience and specialized training and skills for use in district emergency operations.

THE LOCKDOWN DRILL TEAM

During an actual Lockdown, members of the Emergency Response Team may be in classrooms or administrative offices in Lockdown mode and unable to assist with the response.

The Lockdown Drill Team should not include personnel that have specific roles during an actual emergency within that school. Instead, the team might include a school nurse or medical professional, district safety representatives, law enforcement, and administrators from another school.

STAFF NOTIFICATION

When Lockdown drills are first being introduced to a school, it is absolutely okay to tell staff in advance of the drill. There may be staff members adversely affected by surprise drills.

SPECIAL NEEDS CONSIDERATIONS

It is critical to identify any specific issues that may cause challenges for students and/or staff with special needs or disabilities and incorporate appropriate actions for notification prior to drills. It is not recommended that additional assistance be provided in special needs areas for drills, UNLESS this assistance is part of the plan and those resources will be assigned in an actual emergency.

THE PRE-DRILL BRIEFING

Prior to the Lockdown drill, a short planning meeting with the Lockdown Drill Team should occur. The agenda is simple:

- Review the floor plan and team member assignments;
- Expected drill duration;
- The door knock and classroom conversation;
- Potential student or staff distress;
- Ensure law enforcement has access to keys to unlock all doors.

ANNOUNCING THE LOCKDOWN DRILL

When using public address to announce a Lockdown drill, repeat,

"This is a drill. Lockdown. Locks, Lights, Out of Sight.

This is a drill. Lockdown. Locks, Lights, Out of Sight."

It's important announce the word "Drill" first to prevent an immediate reaction to the word Lockdown.

Another way to announce it is:

"We are going to conduct a Lockdown drill.
Please listen for the Lockdown announcement."

CONDUCTING THE DRILL

The Lockdown Drill Team should be broken into groups of two or three members who go to individual classrooms. One of the members acts as a "Scribe" and documents each classroom response. Large schools will need multiple Lockdown Drill Teams in order to complete the drill in a timely fashion.

At the classroom door, team members listen for noise and look through the corridor window for any student or staff visibility or movement. A team member then knocks on the door and requests entry. There should be no response to this request. At this point, a member of the team unlocks the classroom door and announces their name and position. A quick assessment is made by the safety team. The occupants of the room are reminded that they are still in Lockdown and should remain so until they hear an announcement that the drill is completed.

A Lockdown Response Worksheet was created by The "I Love U Guys" Foundation to assist in documenting the Lockdown drills. It can be copied from the following page or downloaded.

WINDOWS

Often there is a conversation about inside and outside windows. Corridor windows are left uncovered so that first responders can see inside the room. Outside windows are left untouched because the threat would be inside the building. There are different preferences regarding window coverings, so please discuss this with your local responders to make sure you're in agreement.

THE CLASSROOM CONVERSATION

Make sure to stake out a few minutes after the room has been checked, and before the release of the drill, to allow for conversation in the classroom.

Typically, this conversation addresses the purpose of the drill, and the observed outcome for that classroom. Additionally, self-evacuation and other life safety strategies can be discussed.

Any issues should be addressed gently but immediately. When possible, have a school counselor available to address any staff or student distress.

THE LOCKDOWN DRILL TEAM DEBRIEF

At the conclusion of the drill, the team should reconvene for a debrief and use this time to review portions of the school safety plan. A good debriefing may reveal some gaps and areas for improvement in the plan.

Any issues should be documented, the safety plan reviewed, and action items identified. An opportunity for all staff to submit information regarding the performance of the drill should be part of the after-action review process.

MATERIALS
And a Note for Your Printer

NOTE TO PRINTERS
All materials are available to download from iloveuguys.org. This material may be duplicated for distribution per "SRP Terms of Use," which reads as follows:

Terms of Use: District/school is responsible for physical material production of any online resources provided by The Foundation. The Foundation does not provide printing services.

What this means: Print these yourself or send them to a printer.

Terms of Use: School District agrees to incorporate the SRP using the terms of art and the associated directives as defined in the Program Description.

What this means: The school, district, agency or organization may place their logo and/or name on printed material to personalize it. They may not substantively change the wording or actions, except as it applies to hazards specific to their region.

ABOUT THE MATERIALS
Most of the materials do not change from one version to the next. Some of them may be marked with a 2025 stamp which shows that they've been reviewed.

PRINTING THE BOOKS
Books have been laid out with a 5 pica (.83") interior margin and a 4 pica (.67") exterior margin to facilitate duplex printing of the materials. Books can be finished using common bindery methods: perfect bind, comb bind, spiral bind, saddle stitch, or punch for a 3-ring binder.

BOOK VERSIONS
The "I Love U Guys" Foundation commits to updating the Standard Response Protocol book versions every two years. All content is reviewed and may or may not change significantly. The previous version will always be available.

SRP K12 2025 Operational Guidance V4.2
Current guidance for schools, districts, departments and agencies. This is a general guide on incorporating and operating the Standard Response Protocol within a school safety plan. V4.2 contains the same information as V4.1, with additional guidance and material.

SRP K12 2023 Operational Guidance V4.1
Guidance for schools, districts, departments and agencies. This is a general guide on incorporating and operating the Standard Response Protocol within a school safety plan.

SRP K12-T 2021 Classroom Instructor Guide
The workbook is designed to assist presenters in learning the SRP presentation.

Accompanying Keynote and PowerPoint presentations are available for download.

SRP PK-2 V2 Curriculum Workbook
This workbook has been produced to help preschool and elementary teachers guide students through the process of learning how to stay safe by engaging in fun activities. It is scheduled to be updated later in 2024.

MATERIALS

INFORMATION FOR PARENTS AND GUARDIANS

Clear communication to parents and guardians about the SRP is essential so they understand the actions your school will be using. By being as clear as possible, you can reduce the amount of stress they might experience for even the small disruptions in a school day.

They need to understand their roles in any incident. The letter-size handout is in PDF format and can be emailed or printed to hand out. It describes what is expected of people in the school, and outlines the roles of the parents and guardians during Secure and Lockdown events.

Schools should outline the methods with which they will be communicating with parents and guardians about any drill or actual incident. It is imperative that parents and guardians keep their contact information up to date with the school and district. Your school or district is welcome to post this on your website for easy access.

Other Languages
The Parent Handout is available in multiple languages. These are produced on request. Requests from schools or districts with a Memorandum of Understanding on file with The Foundation are prioritized.

SRP Parent Handout
2 pages, English language

SRP Parent Handout
2 pages, Spanish language

RED CARD/GREEN CARD

This is for use in an Evacuation Assembly to do a quick assessment of the status of all groups. It is not for classroom use during a Lockdown or Lockdown Drill.

There are three different types for different situations, so choose to use the one that's best for your environment.

After arriving at an Evacuation Assembly and taking roll, the Red/Green Cards are used for administration or first responders to quickly and visually identify the status of the teachers' classes after an evacuation.

The back of all cards have the **Help and OK** images.

Green = All students are accounted for, No immediate help is necessary

Red = Extra or missing students, or vital information must be exchanged

Red/GREEN/Med Card
Red and White Cross (Medical Help) - Immediate medical attention is needed

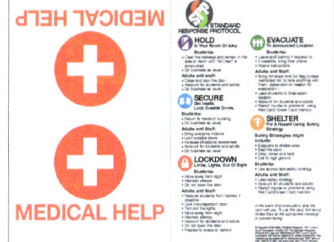

Red/GREEN/Roll Card
This includes a roll sheet for users to record who is in their group.

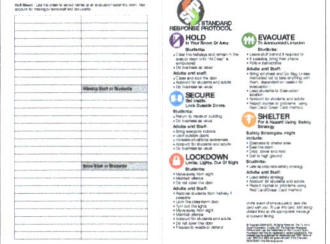

Red/GREEN/Alert Card
The Alert card is used to indicate there is a problem in your group and you need assistance.

MATERIALS

SRP CLASSROOM POSTER

This K12 SRP overview wall poster was created to be printed and placed on walls in order to remind everyone of the different SRP actions and allow teachers to start the conversation about SRP with their students.

Placing posters is an essential step in the full implementation of the SRP. The poster should be displayed in classrooms, near building entries, and at the entrances to the cafeteria, auditorium and the gym. The Shelter hazards and safety strategies can be modified for local conditions.

The poster is available in letter size (8.5 x 11") and tabloid size (11 x 17") in English and Spanish.

The poster is available in multiple languages which are produced on request. Requests from schools or districts with a Memorandum of Understanding on file with The Foundation are prioritized.

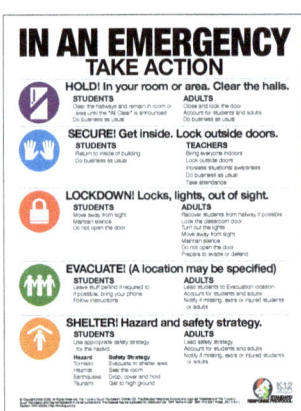 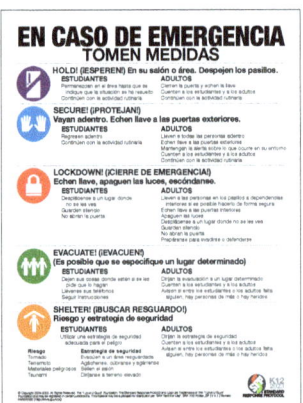

PUBLIC ADDRESS POSTER

The Public Address Poster can be placed near all reasonable public address locations. This is a sample. Your district, department or agency should customize this poster for regional hazards. It is available to download in Microsoft Word for easy editing. The public address is repeated twice each time the public address is performed.

Hold! In your room or area. Clear the halls.

Secure! Get Inside. Lock outside doors.

Lockdown! Locks, Lights, Out of Sight.

Evacuate! To a Location.

Shelter! State the Hazard and Safety Strategy.

STATUS POSTERS

Letter-size posters for use to communicate the status of the school during drills or incidents.

These include posters for two levels of Secure conditions, and a Lockdown Drill Poster.

 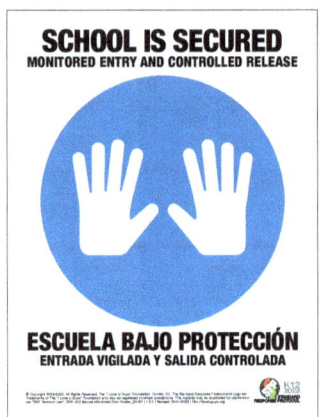

POCKET GUIDE

This is a quick guide to the five actions. It folds to the size of a business card to fit in wallets, pockets, and ID cardholders. It prints on two sides of letter-size paper and there are three to a page.

MATERIALS

ID CARDS
Art for printing onto identification cards is available for slotted and unslotted cards in the standard size of 3.375" x 2.125".

VIDEO TRAINING
There are some videos you can download from iloveuguys.org, or YouTube, to use for training purposes.

Middle/High School Video (7:26)
This is a teenage student speaking with a School Resource Officer about the actions of the SRP. It's appropriate for students in middle school and older.

Lockdown Drill (3:35)
This was recorded during a High School Lockdown drill. It includes interviews with students, and is appropriate for all ages of students.

SRP-2021 What's New (5:43)
This video highlights the changes for SRP 2021, and specifically the change from Lockout to Secure.

SRP Dispatch Roll Call (5:59)
Dispatchers play an integral, yet often overlooked, role in any crisis. This video sheds light on the importance of dispatchers understanding and utilizing the common language of the SRP for effective communications between law enforcement, fire, EMS, and the school or district. Grab 10 minutes during roll call to present this video to dispatchers so they can learn more about the five actions of the SRP, when and why they are used, and what communications will look like for dispatchers.

SRP Patrol Roll Call (4:28)
When schools within your jurisdiction are using the SRP, it is crucial for all first responders to have a comprehensive understanding of the five actions of the SRP in order to understand the status of a crisis at the schools and be able to effectively respond. In this video, our Hollywood voiceover artist gives patrol team members an overview of the SRP and its five actions, and he takes you through real-world scenarios of what this will look like for law enforcement. Show this video at roll call with your officers and discuss it with them to solidify their understanding of the SRP.

FAQ
Frequently Asked Questions

YOU MAY ASK...
Since introducing the Standard Response Protocol in 2009, thousands of districts, departments and agencies have scrutinized, evaluated and ultimately implemented the program. During the process some questions seem to come up often.

Seriously. What does it really cost?
Since its introduction in 2009, public K12 schools, districts, departments and agencies were free to use The "I Love U Guys" Foundation programs at no cost.

In 2015, the Foundation expanded availability, and now offers the programs to any public or private organization at no charge. Download the materials and begin the process.

What about business/church/institution use?
Please look at the materials designed specifically for institutional use on the website: **iloveuguys.org**.

I see you offer training. Do we need to buy training in order to use the program?
No. We've attempted to put enough material online so that schools and law enforcement can successfully implement Foundation programs. We know of thousands of schools across the US and Canada that have implemented the programs using internal resources.

That said, part of our sustainability model relies not just on charitable giving, but on providing training for districts, departments, and agencies. If your organization is interested in Foundation training, please contact us for rates and terms.

What's the difference between Secure and Lockdown again?
The term "Secure " is used when there is a potential threat that can be mitigated by bringing everyone inside. It should be announced with the directive "Get inside. Lock outside doors," which signals to bring people in and lock exterior doors. While it calls for heightened situational awareness, it also allows for indoor activities to continue.

The term "Lockdown" means there is an active or imminent threat inside or nearby requiring immediate protective action. It is followed by the directive "Locks, Lights, Out of Sight" and requires locking classroom doors, turning out the lights, and remaining hidden until first responders arrive.

Effectively if the threat is outside the building, Secure . If the threat is inside the building, Lockdown.

What if the threat is close to the building?
There may be situations where both Secure and Lockdown protocols may be called sequentially. In this case, use Secure to get people inside and lock exterior doors. When the perimeter is Secured, this may become a Lockdown if the threat is persistent and appears to be coming closer. Exterior doors would stay locked.

In Lockdown, you suggest unlocking the outside doors. What's up with that?
No, we don't. We occasionally hear this but our guidance is actually a little different. We suggest not putting anyone at risk by locking or unlocking outside doors. If the doors are locked, leave them locked. Be sure you have a plan that allows first responders to enter the building quickly.

Won't people still come in the building if the outside doors are unlocked during a Lockdown?
Yes, people may be able to enter the building during the window of time between calling a lockdown and the arrival of first responders.

A lockdown is called when there is a life safety threat inside the building. During the development and throughout the lifecycle of the SRP, constant and deliberate scrutiny of all risk/benefit guidance is performed by the Foundation, district and law enforcement representatives. This has resulted in the lockdown guidance provided.

That said, with any guidance provided, we defer to local decisions. If you are a district, please consult with your local law enforcement representatives for final guidance.

I thought I saw Shelter guidance?
When we developed the SRP and released the first version in 2009 we included FEMA guidance regarding the Shelter directive and actions. FEMA changed that guidance in 2014. We are removing specific shelter guidance from our documentation and deferring to the current practices published at **http://fema.gov** as well as your local emergency management guidance.

Can the SRP be used in conjunction with other safety plans?
Yes, absolutely. The SRP is designed as an enhancement to any safety plan. It covers critical incidents by standardizing vocabulary so stakeholders can easily understand the status and respond quickly when an unforeseen event occurs. Comprehensive safety plans will include components such as communications, threat assessment, local hazards, operation continuity and reunification, among other items.

Can I modify materials?
That depends. The core actions and directives must remain intact. These are:

1. Hold "In your room or area. Clear the halls."
2. Secure "Get inside. Locks outside doors"
3. Lockdown "Locks, Lights, Out of Sight"
4. Evacuate followed by the announced location
5. Shelter followed by the announced hazard and safety strategy

Some details may need to be customized to your location. For instance, the public address poster should be modified to include hazards and safety strategies that are specific to your location.

Are the source materials available?
Yes. Some of the materials are available. Original, digital artwork can be provided to organizations that have a signed "Memorandum of Understanding" with The "I Love U Guys" Foundation.

Please note: Currently, original artwork is created in Mac OS X, Pages version 14.x or InDesign 19.x.

Can you send me the materials in Microsoft Word?
The Public Address Poster, and all MOUs and NOIs are produced in Word. The other materials are not. Retaining the graphic integrity of the materials proved beyond our capabilities using Microsoft Word.

Can I really use the materials? What about copyrights and trademarks?
Schools, districts, departments, agencies and organizations are free to use the materials under the "Terms of Use" outlined in this document and in the Memorandum of Understanding.

Do I need to ask permission to use the materials?
No. You really don't need to ask permission. But, it would be great if you let us know that you're using our programs.

Do I have to sign an MOU with The Foundation?
It is not necessary to sign an MOU with the Foundation, but please consider it. The Foundation is committed to providing programs at no cost. Yet, program development, enhancement, and support are cost centers for us. One way we fund those costs is through private grants and funding.

An MOU is a strong demonstration of program validity and assists us with these types of funding requests.

When you submit a completed MOU or NOI, you will be added to our database and notified when updates and new materials are available.

Do I have to send a Notice of Intent?
In the absence of an MOU, a Notice of Intent provides similar value to us regarding demonstrations of program validity to potential funders. Either one means that you will receive notification of updates and new materials.

Do I have to notify you at all that I'm using the SRP?
We often speak with school safety stakeholders who have implemented the SRP but haven't mentioned it to us. Please let us know if your school, district, department or agency is using the SRP.

It is our goal that the SRP becomes the "Gold Standard." The more schools, districts, departments and agencies that we can show are using the program, the greater the chance of achieving our goal of having clear communication in a crisis.

Can I put our logo on your materials?
Yes. But with some caveats. If you are a school, district, department or agency you may include your logo on posters and handouts. If you are a commercial enterprise, please contact us in advance with the intended usage.

In some states, we have co-branding agreements with "umbrella" organizations (school district insurance pools, school safety centers, etc.). In those states, we ask that you also include the umbrella organization's branding.

We would like to put the materials on our website.
Communication with your community is important. While you are free to place any material on your website, it's preferable that you link to the materials from our website. The reason for this is to allow us to track material usage. We can then use these numbers when we seek funding.

But, don't let that be a show-stopper. If your IT group prefers, just copy the materials to your site.

Does the SRP replace other individual response programs?
The SRP serves as an all-hazards, institutional response to anything that can happen at a school, and includes many options. Individual response programs often only identify options for the active assailant situation.

The SRP does not negate individual response training. In fact, you may find the different trainings can enhance each other and provide multiple responses.

DRILLS
FEMA Guidance

APPENDIX A - FEMA GUIDANCE

FEMA provides a description of each exercise and drill. The following information is from FEMA resources. The chart on the right page is their Building Block chart, and the descriptions here are how FEMA describes what each one entails, and the expected outcomes.

For in-depth learning, see IS-120.C: An Introduction to Exercises: (**https://training.fema.gov/is/courseoverview.aspx?code=is-120.c**)

DISCUSSION-BASED EXERCISES

SEMINAR
Seminars orient participants to or provide an overview into strategies, plans, policies, or procedures. Seminars can be valuable when an entity is developing new plans or making changes to existing plans or procedures.

Goals
- Orient participants to new or existing plans, policies, or procedures
- Research or assess inter-agency capabilities or inter-jurisdictional operations
- Construct a common framework of understanding

Characteristics
- Casual atmosphere
- Minimal time constraints
- Lecture-based

WORKSHOP
Workshops are more structured than seminars. Participant attendance and collaboration from relevant stakeholders is essential to obtaining consensus and producing effective plans, procedures, and agreements.

Goals
- Develop a written product as a group, in coordinated activities
- Obtain consensus
- Collect or share information

Characteristics
- Broad attendance by relevant stakeholders
- Conducted based on clear objectives/goals
- More participant discussion than lecture-based seminar
- Frequently uses break-out sessions to explore parts of an issue with similar groups

Outcomes
- Emergency Operations Plans (EOPs)
- Mutual Aid Agreements
- Standard Operations Procedures (SOPs)

TABLETOP EXERCISE (TTX)
Tabletop exercises facilitate conceptual understanding, identify strengths, and areas for improvements, and/or achieving changes in perceptions. Participants are encouraged to problem-solve together through in-depth discussion. An effective TTX comes from active participants and their assessment of recommended revisions to current plans, policies, and procedures. It is important to have a facilitator keep the participants focused on the exercise objectives.

Goals
- Enhance general awareness
- Enhance roles and responsibility understanding
- Validate plans and procedures
- Rehearse concepts and/or assess types of systems in a defined incident

Characteristics
- Requires an experienced facilitator
- In-depth discussion
- Low stress, problem-solving environment

GAME
A simulation of operations that often involves two or more teams, usually in a competitive environment, using rules, data, and procedures designed to depict an actual or hypothetical situation. Identifying critical decision-making points is a major factor in the success of games.

Goals
- Explore decision-making processes and consequences
- Conduct "what-if" analyses of existing plans
- Evaluate existing and potential strategies
- Characteristics
- No actual resources used
- Often involves two or more teams
- Includes models and simulations on increasing complexity as the game progresses
- May include pre-scripted messages

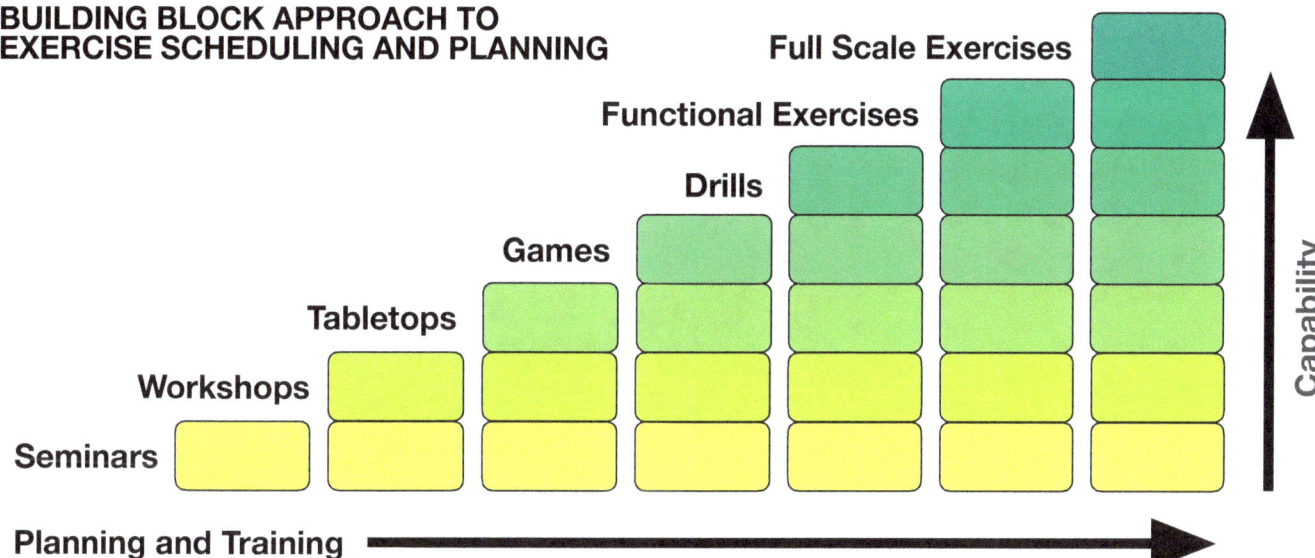

OPERATIONS-BASED EXERCISES

DRILL
A drill is a coordinated, supervised activity usually employed to validate a specific function or capability in a single agency organization. Drills are commonly used to provide training on tasks specific to new equipment or procedures, to introduce or validate procedures, or practice and maintain current skills.

Goals
- Provide training on new equipment
- Evaluate new procedures, policies, and/or equipment
- Practice and maintain skills
- Prepare for more complex exercises

Characteristics
- Immediate feedback
- Realistic but isolated environment

FUNCTIONAL EXERCISE (FE)
These are designed to validate and evaluate capabilities, multiple functions and/or sub-functions, or interdependent groups of functions. FEs are typically focused on exercising plans, policies, procedures, and staff members involved in management, direction, command, and control functions.

Goals
- Validate and evaluate capabilities
- Focused on plans, policies, and procedures

Characteristics
- Conducted in a realistic, real-time simulated environment
- Simulated deployment of resources and personnel
- Use of SimCell and Master Scenario Events List (MSEL)
- Include controller and evaluators

FULL-SCALE EXERCISE (FSE)
Full-scale exercises (FSE) are high-stress, multi-agency, multi-jurisdictional activities designed to test coordinated responses and rapid problem-solving skills. These are the most complex, resource-intensive, and possibly expensive exercises.

Goals
- Demonstrate roles and responsibilities as addressed in plans and procedures
- Coordinate between multiple agencies, organizations, and jurisdictions

Characteristics
- High-stress environment
- Rapid problem solving
- Critical thinking
- Conducted in a realistic, real-time environment to mirror a real incident
- Mobilization of units, personnel, and equipment

THE STANDARD REUNIFICATION METHOD

SRM V3

REUNIFY

A Practical Method to Unite Students with Parents After an Evacuation or Crisis.
The "I Love U Guys" Foundation

STANDARD REUNIFICATION METHOD™

SRM V3 CHANGE HISTORY

AUTHOR/CONTRIBUTOR	VERSION	REVISION DATE	REVISION COMMENTARY
John-Michael Keyes	0.9.0	9/17/2011	Preliminary Draft
John-Michael Keyes	0.9.1	10/1/2011	First Final Contest Revision
Ellen Stoddard-Keyes	0.9.2	10/16/2011	Preliminary Edits
Lee Shaughnessy	0.9.3	10/26/2011	Preliminary Edits
Joseph Majsak	1.0	11/16/2011	Continuity and Final Edits
John-Michael Keyes	1.1	6/8/2016	Additional Content
John-Michael Keyes Will Schwall Michelle Brady Russ Deffner Carolyn Mears	2.0	3/2/2017	Reunifier replaces Runner Additional Content Edits
Kevin Burd, Priority of Life Ellen Stoddard-Keyes Allyson Jones Melissa A. Reeves, Ph.D, NCSP, LCMHC Bill Godfrey, C3 Pathways	3.0	3/27/2023	Updates and Edits Update ICS / HSEEP Compatibility Update Communication Recommendations NASP Guidance Violent Event Guidance

The Standard Reunification Method
A Practical Method to Unite Students with Parents After an Evacuation or Crisis
The "I Love U Guys" Foundation
Version 3.0
ISBN - 978-1-951260-12-5

© Copyright 2009 - 2024, All rights reserved. The "I Love U Guys" Foundation. SRP, The Standard Response Protocol, SRM, Standard Reunification Method, and I Love U Guys are Trademarks of The "I Love U Guys" Foundation and may registered in certain jurisdictions.

DEDICATION
The "I Love U Guys" Foundation dedicates this book to the many people who have invested time, knowledge and caring toward the art of safely and responsibly reuniting students, guardians and families when daily routines are disrupted.

FORWARD
The concept for the Standard Reunification Method (SRM) isn't new. There are many resources available to design a well-run reunification, however few have all the parts in one place. The SRM is a synthesis of common practices in use at a number of districts, departments, and agencies, as well as guidance provided by a variety of federal governmental agencies.

The evolution of SRM has included reviews, comments, and suggestions from a number of practitioners. As of 2023, the SRM has been subjected to tactical scrutiny by hundreds of law enforcement agencies and operational review and adoption by thousands of schools.

ACKNOWLEDGMENTS
The "I Love U Guys" Foundation is primarily grateful to Will Schwall, Emergency Manager, Hays County Sheriff's Office, San Marcos, Texas, for the structure and organization of the materials, and Michelle Brady, Emergency Planning Coordinator, Hillsboro School District, Hillsboro, Oregon, for inspiring the job action sheets.

INPUT AND GUIDANCE
We are grateful to the following people who helped with additional, indirect guidance for the Standard Reunification Method:

Pat Hamilton – Chief Operating Officer, Adams 12 Five Star Schools, Ret.

Bill Godfrey - C3 Pathways
https://www.c3pathways.com

Kevin Burd, Priority of Life Training and Consulting
https://priorityoflife.org

ADJUNCT INSTRUCTORS
The Foundation has a growing pool of skilled and trained instructors who conduct trainings around the country on a part time basis, bringing their expertise and knowledge to the table. They bring back information, and we work together to stay current and improve the programs.

CONTACT INFORMATION
The I Love U Guys Foundation can be reached online at iloveuguys.org.

Email: srm@iloveuguys.org

The "I Love U Guys" Foundation

P.O. Box 489, Placitas, NM 87043

REQUEST FOR COMMENT
The Standard Reunification Method is a synthesis of common practices in use at a number of districts, departments, and agencies, as well as guidance provided by a variety of federal governmental agencies.

The evolution of SRM has included reviews, comments, and suggestions from a number of practitioners. As of 2023, the SRM has been subjected to tactical scrutiny by hundreds of law enforcement agencies and operational review and adoption by thousands of schools.

Suggestions for modification can be made via email at srm_rfc@iloveuguys.org. Please include contact information, district, department, or agency, including daytime phone.

MISSION
The "I Love U Guys" Foundation was created to restore and protect the joy of youth through educational programs and positive actions in collaboration with families, schools, communities, organizations, and government entities.

THE "I LOVE U GUYS" FOUNDATION
On September 27th, 2006 a gunman entered Platte Canyon High School in Bailey, Colorado, held seven girls hostage, and ultimately shot and killed Emily Keyes. During the time she was held hostage, Emily sent her parents text messages... "I love you guys" and "I love u guys. k?"

Emily's kindness, spirit, fierce joy, and the dignity and grace that followed this tragic event define the core of The "I Love U Guys" Foundation.

COMMITMENT
There are several things we are committed to. The most important thing we can do is offer our materials at no cost to schools, districts, departments, agencies, and organizations. The reason we are able to continue to provide this service is due, in part, to the generosity of our donors and Mission Partners (see the Partner with Love section at **iloveuguys.org**). The "I Love U Guys" Foundation works very hard to keep our costs down as well as any costs associated with our printed materials. Donor and Mission Partner support allows us to stretch those dollars and services even more. Your gift, no matter the size, helps us achieve our mission. Your help makes a difference to the students, teachers, first responders, and the communities in which we live and work.

WARNINGS AND DISCLAIMER
Every effort has been made to make this book as complete and accurate as possible, but no warranty or fitness is implied. The information provided is on an "as is" basis. Please visit our website (**iloveuguys.org**) for detailed information.

COPYRIGHTS AND TRADEMARKS
In order to protect the integrity and consistency of The Standard Reunification Method, The "I Love U Guys" Foundation exercises all protection under copyright and trademark. Use of this material is governed by the Terms of Use or a Commercial Licensing Agreement.

COMMERCIAL LICENSING
Incorporating the SRM into a commercial product, like software or publication, requires a commercial license. Please contact The "I Love U Guys" Foundation for more information and costs.

ABOUT THIS BOOK
In 2012, The "I Love U Guys" Foundation introduced the Standard Reunification Method. At the time, we saw a void in school safety planning regarding student/parent reunification after an incident. We were certain this was a true need, but few schools or districts actually had reunification plans and practices in place. Fewer still had actually drilled or practiced.

Was it truly a need? The answer lies in the widespread adoption of the SRM. Since 2012, thousands of schools in the US and Canada have implemented the Standard Reunification Method as a means to safely reunite students and families after a crisis.

Recovery starts before the crisis begins. Reunification is one step in that recovery.

This is Version 3.0 of the Standard Reunification Method. But notice, we use the word method. Not protocol. Not procedure. Method.

What that means is that we provide you with some tactics. Things we know. But the incident, your reunification site, and your environment, will ultimately dictate what you do.

Please, in your planning, if you see something here that doesn't seem to work in your environment, figure out what does. Let us know.

The term "parent" is intended to be inclusive of any adult caregiver who acts as a guardian and provides care for a student. This includes a biological or adoptive parent, guardian, legal custodian, or caregiver with legal authority to make decisions on behalf of the child.

ABOUT SRM V3
Version 3 contains expanded guidance, closer adherence to FEMA Incident Command System, and compatibility with HSEEP (Homeland Security Exercise and Evaluation Program) 2020.

Although SRM Version 2 is still valid, The I Love U Guys Foundation recommends updating to the newer version when possible.

THE "I LOVE U GUYS" FOUNDATION MOU
Some schools, districts, departments, and agencies may also desire a formalized Memorandum of Understanding (MOU) with The "I Love U Guys" Foundation. For a current version of the MOU, please visit **iloveuguys.org**.

The purpose of this MOU is to define the responsibilities of each party and provide scope, and clarity of expectations. It affirms the agreement of stated protocol by schools, districts, departments, and agencies. It also confirms the online availability of the Foundation's materials.

An additional benefit for the Foundation is in seeking funding. Some private grantors view the MOU as a demonstration of program effectiveness.

TERMS OF USE

Schools, districts, departments, agencies, and organizations may use these materials, at no cost, under the following conditions:

1. Materials are not re-sold.
2. Notification of use is provided to The "I Love U Guys" Foundation through one of the following:
   2.1 Email notice of use to
      srm@iloveuguys.org
   2.2 Memorandum of Understanding
3. The following modification to the parent handouts and reunification cards are allowable:
   3.1 Localization

FAIR USE POLICY

These materials are for educational and informational purposes only and may contain copyrighted material the use of which has not always been specifically authorized by the copyright owner. In accord with our nonprofit mission, we are making such material available for the public good to restore and protect the joy of youth through educational programs and positive actions in collaboration with families, schools, communities, organizations, and government entities.

The "I Love U Guys" Foundation IRS 501(c)3 est. 2006 asserts this constitutes a 'fair use' of any such copyrighted material as provided in Section 107 of the US Copyright Law. In accordance with Title 17 U.S.C. Section 107, these materials are distributed without profit to those who have expressed a prior interest in receiving the included information for criticism, comment, news reporting, teaching, scholarship, education, and research.

If you wish to use copyrighted material from this site for purposes of your own that go beyond fair use, you must obtain permission from the copyright owner.

If your copyrighted material appears in our materials and you disagree with our assessment that it constitutes 'fair use,' contact us.

PRIVACY POLICY

When you agree to the Terms of Use by sending an MOU, your contact information will be entered into a database. You will receive notifications when there are updates and/or new materials. You will have the opportunity to opt in to receive periodic blog posts and newsletters via email.

Our Commitment to Program Users: We will not sell, share or trade names, contact, or personal information with any other entity, nor send mailings to our donors on behalf of other organizations. This policy applies to all information received by The "I Love U Guys" Foundation, both online and off-line, as well as any electronic, written, or oral communications. Please see iloveuguys.org for the full Privacy text.

"Cops own the crime. Fire owns the flames. Schools own the kids."

"But Paramedics own the patient."

And that may be an area of conflict during an incident.

Your reunification plans and methods must be communicated with first responders prior to an incident.

REUNIFICATION

The nation has experienced high-profile acts of school violence. In response to this and the everyday types of crises, The "I Love U Guys" Foundation develops programs to help districts, departments, and agencies respond.

One critical aspect of crisis response is accountable reunification of students with their parents or guardians in the event a controlled release is necessary. The Standard Reunification Method provides school and district safety teams with proven methods for planning, practicing, and achieving a successful reunification. Keep in mind, though, that this is an evolving process. While there is a smattering of science in these methods, tailoring these to your school is certainly an artful process. Site-specific considerations will dictate how these practices can be integrated into school and district safety plans. Successful planning and implementation will also demand partnerships with all responding agencies participating in a crisis response.

ADAMS 12, FIVE STAR SCHOOLS METHOD

The methods detailed in the first version of the Standard Reunification Method are based on the practices developed at the Adams 12, Five Star School District, Thornton, Colorado, by Pat Hamilton, Chief Operating Officer, and also at Jefferson County School District, Golden, Colorado, by John McDonald, Executive Director of Security and Emergency Planning.

Since its introduction in 2012, other districts and agencies have also contributed.

The core concept of the Adams 12 Reunification Method rests on accountability achieved through a process based on managing the physical location of students, staff, and incoming parents. The process also uses perforated cards. These cards are completed by parents or guardians at the reunification site. The cards are separated at the perforation, and a reunifier retrieves the child.

OBJECTIVES

The objective of this manual is to help districts develop, train, and mobilize a district reunification team, and implement tangible, on-site, and off-site reunification plans. Inherent in this objective is creating or strengthening partnerships with responding agencies – police, fire, and medical. By having school and district personnel build a well-designed draft plan, it becomes easier to engage the responders and other key participants in the planning process. During this process, a core philosophy is essential:

Cops own the crime.
Fire owns the flames.
Schools own the kids.
Paramedics own the patient.

Additionally, performing a successful reunification is much more likely when drills are conducted in advance of an event. Tabletop exercises and live exercises should be scheduled and performed.

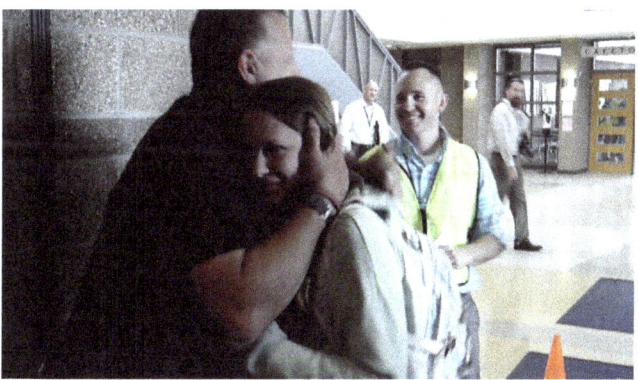

WHAT DOES IT COST?

Implementing the Standard Reunification Method concepts and planning stages take a certain amount of time. But in the grand scheme of school safety, the level of effort is modest. There will be some staff hours committed to the planning, training, and practice of these concepts. There will be some cost in printing, and in creating both the ROK boxes (Reunification Operation Kits) and the classroom "go kits" necessary for successful reunification.

"Go kits" are the bags or folders that teachers need in their classrooms during any type of event. They often include class rosters, tissues, space blankets, candy for low blood sugar, and other items specific to the location and students. ROK Boxes are typically maintained at the district level and contain everything necessary for the reunification team to function.

Visit iloveuguys.org to find links for all materials found in the ROK box. Since some of this activity is happening at the district level, the cost of the kits can be spread among all of the schools in the district.

WHEN TO INITIATE A REUNIFICATION

Initiating a reunification can be a result of anything abnormal at the school that renders it unsafe to stay in, or something in the area such as a power or phone outage, weather event, hazmat incident, bomb threats, criminal activity in the area, or active violence at the school.

In some cases, it may be only a partial student population reunification. For instance, criminal activity in the area might result in reunifying students who walk to and from school. In other instances, reunification of the entire student population may be necessary for things such as a gas leak in the school or a violent event.

WHY BOTHER?

Crisis recovery starts before the crisis, not after. Simply "winging it" when reuniting ignores not only the mental health demands that accompany a crisis, but the responsibility of the school and the district to maintain the chain of custody for every student.

No school is immune to stuff hitting the proverbial fan. Wild land or structural fires, hazardous materials, floods, tornadoes, blizzards, power outages, tsunamis, bomb threats, acts of violence, acts of terror... these just start the list of events that may necessitate a controlled reunification and release for a school or district.

A predetermined, practiced reunification method ensures the reunification process will not further complicate what may already be a chaotic, anxiety-filled scene. In fact, putting an orderly reunification plan into action will help prevent emotions from escalating at the site.

There is an added bonus to implementing the Standard Reunification Method. Going through the planning and training process may help strengthen district relationships with first responders. Often law enforcement is active in partnering with schools and districts. Less often is the fire department. The SRM may be a vector for strengthening relationships with fire agencies as well.

THE PROCESS IN A NUTSHELL

The materials in this manual provide the fundamentals for a comprehensive district plan. The beauty of the Standard Reunification Method is its simplicity.

- Establish a parent/guardian check-in location.
- Deliver the students to an assembly area or a transportation area beyond the field of vision of parents/guardians.
- Conduct accountability, or attendance, of who is at the assembly area (student and staff).
- Once students are on-site, notify parents/guardians of the location.
- "Greeters" hand parents/guardians a Reunification Card, and help them understand the process.
- The parent/guardian completes the card and brings it to the check-in area. The procedure allows parents/guardians to self-sort during check-in, streamlining the process.
- Parent/guardian identification is verified. The card is split at the perforation, and the parent/guardian receives the bottom portion.
- Parent/guardian brings that to an area outside the student assembly area and hands it to a "Reunifier."
- The "Reunifier" recovers a student from the assembly area and delivers them to the parent/guardian.
- Controlled lines of sight allow for an orderly flow, and issues can be handled with less drama and anxiety.
- Medical, notification, or investigative contingencies are anticipated.
- Pedestrian "flows" are created so lines don't cross.
- In the end, successful reunification is about managing the student and parent experience.

COMMON QUESTIONS

Who is allowed to pick up students?

This comes down to a local school or district policy. Some schools allow anyone on the emergency contact form to pick up the child. Others limit it to only primary guardians if the reunification is due to a violent event. Your organization will have to think through the process and develop a local policy.

What about kids with multiple guardians, homes, or from multiple families?

It will be essential for schools to communicate with all guardians who may pick up a child. This becomes complicated when kids live in different homes depending on the day. You will also run into a situation where one guardian arrives before the other, picks up the child, and never communicates with the other guardians. The school will have to notify the later arriving guardians once they get to the check-in area that the child has already been picked up.

WHY USE CARDS?

Many schools use electronic rosters or campus information systems. Wouldn't that be easier? The reality is a little different. First and foremost is access to data. Foundation research indicates that in any high profile incident, and even many local ones, internet, and cell service become intermittent or even unresponsive. Often school WiFi is impacted as well.

THE CARD

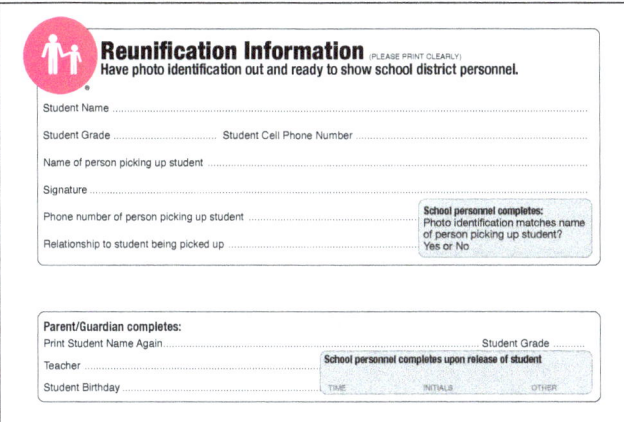

The Reunification Card does a ton of work. Its primary function is to provide accountability, so one student per card is recommended. It also helps with the parent experience. It gives the parent/guardian something to do while they are waiting in line. The card is perforated and gives parents a sense of progress as they go through the process. The main objective is to keep parents/guardians calm and organized while they wait. Let the card do this work for you.

A LITTLE SOCIAL ENGINEERING

A reunification typically occurs because of a crisis or emergency. Consequently, not just students and parents /guardians are trying to function at elevated stress levels; staff, their families, and other first responders also feel the strain.

By having a defined process with signage, cards, branding, procedures, and protocols, the school presents an organized, calm face to all involved. Fear or uncertainty often results from the unknown. By adopting, communicating, and practicing a "known" procedure, the school removes some of that uncertainty.

The cards also bring anxiety down a notch. Asking a parent/guardian to complete the form is a familiar activity and will demand they slow down and perform a cognitive action, "Here, read the instructions on the back, and we'll get things started," might be the first step in lowering blood pressure.

ACCOUNTABILITY: THE ONE NON-NEGOTIABLE

The entire process of reunification, much like any other crisis response method that is based on the National Incident Management System (NIMS) and uses the Incident Command System (ICS), can and should be modified to fit the needs of your local organization. Names and titles can be changed based on what works for you. Ensure all responding agencies understand and are aware of the terminology.

The one thing that cannot be modified is the need for 100% accountability of your students and staff. You absolutely must know who is at the reunification site and who is not. Understand that you may not know the exact location of everyone. This is especially true in a violent event where many will self-evacuate. However, by identifying who is at the impacted site, who evacuated via transportation, and who arrived at the reunification site, you will be able to determine who is present at the reunification site and who is missing.

The accountability process could look like this: During the evacuation phase of an incident, teachers take attendance of their students. This attendance is collected to include staff members, and gives you the number of staff and students you have at the impacted site. If you started the day with 300 total students and staff and you account for 278 during an evacuation, you now know that you need to locate 22 individuals. You should also be able to identify who those missing individuals are. Remember, just because they are not present does not mean they are injured or deceased, as many people will self-evacuate. You will now know that you must maintain the accountability of 278 individuals as they are transported from the impacted site to the reunification site. This information must be communicated to the incident commander at the reunification site and passed along to the student assembly supervisor. Once the students and staff begin to arrive at the reunification site, they will be accounted for by their student assembly supervisor or an accountant assigned to them. If it was not already done, a name-by-name roster should be developed at this point. You absolutely must know the name of each person who has arrived at the reunification site. Once all 278 individuals arrive, you now know that no more transportation is coming from the impacted site. Be sure to confirm this with the impacted site transport team. The name-by-name roster can then be duplicated, one copy stays with the assembly area supervisor, and a second copy goes to the accountant at the parent check-in area. By using this process, you will now know if a student is at the reunification site when their parent or guardian checks in.

NOT SO WEIRD ADVICE

At first blush, this bit of advice may sound weird to educators: "Check out FEMA. Go to http://training.fema.gov and complete the online training for IS-100.C Introduction to Incident Command System." The course takes about an hour and a half to complete and introduces some basic emergency response principles.

Here's why this advice isn't as weird as it sounds. Every responding agency that partners with schools uses "Incident Command" during a crisis. The Incident Command System (ICS) is a response method that determines the role of everyone responding to a crisis and defines a shared vocabulary and shared expectations of behavior.

District and school safety teams need this shared vocabulary when interacting with first responders during a crisis. Equally important is that, when meeting with first responders, having the concepts and vocabulary of ICS removes some of the language barriers. It also shows a commitment to success that departments and agencies will appreciate.

Finally, understanding ICS concepts allows school or district leadership to become a part of the response structure rather than victims or unused assets. It opens the door to a true unified command where school or district leaders can operate shoulder to shoulder with fire, police, EMS, and other public safety leaders.

INCIDENT COMMAND SYSTEM

Whether it is a human-caused or natural crisis, or an act of violence in the school, law enforcement, fire, and medical teams will be involved in the reunification process. Learning to understand and speak a common language as well as being familiar with their procedures is imperative to a successful outcome. With that in mind, district and school safety teams must understand and use the Incident Command System.

The Incident Command System can also be used for pre-planned, non-emergency occasions, such as sporting events or large gatherings. All the tasks that need to be completed before and during the event can be put into the ICS structure. The structure provides a way to better organize tasks and personnel.

PRIORITIES, OBJECTIVES, STRATEGIES, AND TACTICS

A valuable FEMA resource is the Incident Action Planning Guide, and it's a good start in understanding how first responders manage an incident.

From a school or district perspective, it's important to understand that the Incident Commander has an expectation that to be useful during the event, the school or district personnel need to have some experience with incident command.

If the school or district personnel don't exhibit any knowledge of the process, their input may be marginalized.

ARTICULATE YOUR P.O.S.T.

The first step in incident management is defining the priorities, objectives, strategies, and tactics that will be used during the incident. While each one will be unique, there are considerations that can be addressed in advance.

Priorities:
- Student and staff safety and well-being.
- Student and staff whereabouts and condition.
- Starting the recovery process.

Objectives:
- Every student has been accounted for.
- Every staff member has been accounted for.
- Every student still in the school's control is reunited with their parent or guardian.

Strategies:
- The Standard Reunification Method

Tactics:
- Tactics will vary based on the event and the environment, but look at the typical reunification lifecycles on page 16 for a jump start.

The next pages describe the structure of the Incident Command System and how it functions in schools and districts.

Following that, there are examples of what the roles might look like during different types of reunifications.

INCIDENT COMMAND ROLES

These are the different roles people will take during a reunification. When assigning roles for planning purposes, identify the strengths and skills that staff have, and assign them to roles they are best suited to perform. Assign backup staff for each role in case of absences.

On the following pages, various types of reunifications are described. There are explanations of unique considerations for each type of reunification, and how the groups can be activated and used.

Incident Commander

A school Principal is very likely to be the initial Incident Commander. When something unexpected happens (call it an incident) which changes the daily routine, they assess the situation and determine what actions need to be taken. When it will require a responsible reunification of students with parents or guardians, a number of steps are taken.

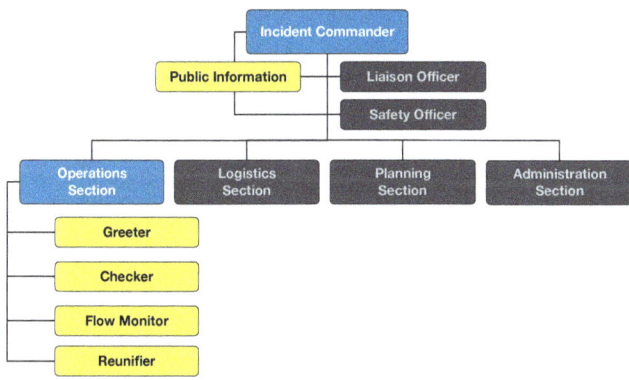

The Incident Commander coordinates Priorities, Objectives, Strategies, and Tactics for an accountable and organized reunification of students with parents/guardians. They decide which key staff stakeholders will be needed, and ensure that notification has been made to them for activation. They will establish security measures for everyone in the school.

However, they do not do it alone. While the Incident Commander is the central point of contact, they are eventually surrounded by a team of support. As people arrive to assist, they assign them to manage specific areas as necessary based on the type of incident. They will assign command staff, who fill very specific roles, as well as section chiefs. The typical sections of the incident command system are Operations, Planning, Logistics, and Administration.

Command Staff

The command staff assists the Incident Commander with communications, safety oversight (to make sure you do not end up with another incident within your incident), and a liaison to ensure integration with other organizations.

Section Chiefs

Section Chiefs, often referred to as the General Staff, report directly to the Incident Commander. They subdivide the incident and assign additional personnel as needed to achieve their objectives. Some, such as Finance/Administration, won't need to be staffed at all during a school-based incident.

Example: In an on-site reunification for a non-violent incident, the Incident Commander assigns an Operations Section Chief who oversees the people conducting the reunification. The reunification team provides Section Chiefs with status and resource information, who in turn report to the Incident Commander. The number of subordinates a school needs will depend on how many students they need to reunite. In a large reunification, the Operations Chief may assign Leads for each group, and the Leads will report to the Chief.

This example assumes that the students are in a main assembly area with their classes, and supervised by their teacher. The decision to engage Logistics or Planning is made by the Incident Commander. If they see a need to acquire or provide supplies such as water or snacks, they might assign someone to Logistics to handle that. In non-violent events, these roles can usually be filled by school staff or may not be needed.

Span of Control

The term "span of control" refers to how many people a single individual can supervise. The recommended span of control is one person supervising no more than seven people, with two to five being the ideal number.

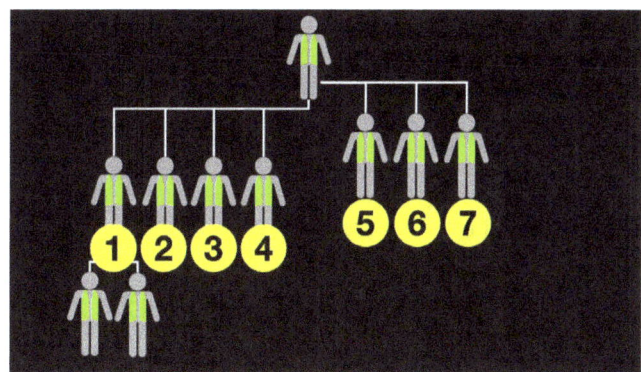

People in various roles will report to the person who is assigned as their commander/supervisor. This keeps communication clear and allows for accurate responses.

It is important to note that the ICS structure is not set in stone. It is adaptable, and jobs, names, and section responsibilities can be adjusted to fit the needs of your organization and location. It is imperative, however, that if changes are made to the traditional model, they are articulated to other local authorities and you practice regularly with them to ensure everyone is on the same page.

COMMUNICATION

In any type of event, clear and well-planned communication is essential to providing the right information while mitigating the stress of the situation. Depending on the type of incident, you might have only minutes to prepare a statement and communicate it to the appropriate people.

Communication with parents and guardians is critical to the reunification process. Once students and staff are at the reunification site and you are ready to begin the reunification process, a multi-channel message is sent to parents and/or guardians regarding where reunification will take place and what they need to bring with them.

PUBLIC INFORMATION OFFICER (PIO)

The role of Public Information Officer is filled by a staff member who usually handles outward communication. No matter how small the incident, the fact that a school day has been disrupted means they are obligated to keep parents and the public informed of the status of the situation.

It is critical for the school and district to ask parents and guardians to update their contact information routinely.

Parents and/or guardians are contacted using the communication method that's best for their school community. Use a push method (text, email, phone) and a passive method such as posting on social media.

Throughout the year, routinely ask parents to update their contact information, and ask them to appoint a trusted friend or neighbor as a backup contact. That is especially important when parents might have a job that restricts their ability to leave, or be available by phone, or requires a long commute.

Joint Information Center

The physical location of the JIC will be determined by the Incident Commander in consultation with the Lead PIO. It is common to locate the JIC away from the crisis site to ensure access to reliable utilities (power, phone, Internet, etc.) and help minimize press congregating at the crisis site.

This can be busy and focused. It will include a few resources who will be working together to deliver clear and consistent messaging as approved by the Incident Commander.

Unless a backup plan for internet service is in place at the crisis site, internet will fail quickly. This affects security cameras and phones if they are VoIP (Voice over Internet Protocol) based.

CHANNELS

Decide which methods of communication are the best fit for your community. This depends on your community's internet bandwidth, cell phone service, and other preferences. Whatever you choose needs to be reliable, fast, and reach a high percentage of community members quickly. Document who on the Communication Team has access to update each channel.

Also, think about which channels are used regularly for day-to-day messaging, like emails and texts. When sending out messages regarding reunification, consider using alternative methods such as text and phone, and your student management system, which may not be used as frequently. Doing so will alert the recipients that this is not the regular, daily email but something more important.

HEALTH PROFESSIONALS

Many schools have mental health professionals as part of their team, and they can be an incredible asset during any type of reunification. An evacuation and reunification can cause stress or anxiety regardless of the reason it was conducted. Therefore, it is important that mental health professionals are on-site and ready to assist.

During a larger reunification, and especially for those occurring due to a violent event, a district-level mental health supervisor should be put in place to oversee mental health services at the reunification site. This Supervisor should work with the incident command staff to ensure mental health services are available for students and staff. Oftentimes those can be placed in or near the student assembly area. Additionally, mental health professionals need to be made available for parents/guardians who are waiting in line. Finally, they should also be at the check-in area to assist families who are notified their student is not at the reunification site.

SCHOOL-BASED MENTAL PREPARATION

A tabletop exercise is a great start; basically, it's a brainstorming session. Your Communication Team talks through possible scenarios and formulates messaging accordingly. They must think about what immediate information is necessary, how to follow up, and who they will need to speak with/follow to receive trusted updates.

Use the 27/9/3 rule during message preparation. This is a very basic recommendation and suggests using a total of 27 words, which can be spoken in about nine seconds, containing three or fewer key points.

The team should pre-script some basic messages that may be sent out with blank spaces for details like time and date. Having these pre-approved and available will aid the team later if they're under stress or time constraints.

THE DISTRICT REUNIFICATION TEAM

Reunification will take place for a variety of reasons. It's a good bet that at some point today a school somewhere is having to conduct a reunification of students with their appropriate caregivers. Most often, reunification will be needed for non-traumatic, non-violent events, such as a power outage, heating loss, or a weather-related event. In these cases, the school typically handles the reunification duties on their own with little to no outside support. However, during larger, more complex incidents, district support will be needed to assist the schools.

Off-site reunification on the other hand will most likely require District resources, and it is a good practice to have a central Reunification Team staffed by District personnel. There are several reasons for this:

- Training can be more readily coordinated;
- Experienced teams are more proficient;
- School-based teams may initially be unavailable.

Smaller districts may recruit from various school administrators to populate the team. Extremely small districts may recruit volunteers from the community to staff the Reunification Team. A good rule of thumb for team size is five people, plus one per 100 students.

Once the staff is at the reunification site, there are roles they will assume for setup, breakdown, and the actual reunification.

REUNIFICATION ROLES AND DUTIES

The following outlines the roles and duties of the Reunification Team. Not all these roles need to be filled for every reunification. For detailed tasks, see the Job Action Sheets found at iloveuguys.org.

Note: Districts may adjust the duties for some roles based on preferences and staffing.

Accountant: Assemble rosters of who is on site and can assist in identifying missing students or staff. In a very small reunification, one person can fill the role of Accountant and Checker.

Checker: Verify ID and confirm the person is on the emergency contact roster. Direct parents to the accountant or the Reunification Area.

Check-in Area Supervisor: Establish and manage the check-in process. Supervise checkers and accountants.

Class Leaders: These are Teachers and Staff who arrive with students and remain in the Student Assembly Area to manage students. Additional people may be assigned to this task.

Communications: Facilitate radio and other communication needs. May be combined with the PIO.

Exit Accountant: Collect bottom slip of reunification card and check students out once reunified. Can be combined with Exit Director role.

Exit Director: The final person students and parents/guardians see during the reunification process. Their role is to be a friendly face who offers a wave or hug. The school principal often fills this role. Can be combined with Exit Accountant.

Facilities: Coordinate any physical plant needs.

Finance/Administration Chief: Establish and manage administrative staff.

Flow Monitor: Assist with guiding traffic flow and assisting parents/guardians as needed.

Greeter: Help coordinate the parent lines. Tell parents about the process. Help verify parents without ID. Your most friendly staff members are good in this role.

Greeter Supervisor: Establish and manage the greeting area, Supervises Greeters.

Liaison Officer: Communicate with Fire, Medical, or Law Enforcement.

Logistics Chief: Establish and manage logistical staff.

Medical Staff: These are nurses or EMS personnel on-site to assist with physical and mental health issues.

Mental Health Supervisor: Oversee the coordination of mental health practitioners from a variety of agencies.

Nutrition Services: Provide snacks and water.

Operations Chief: Establish and manage operational staff.

Planning Chief: Establish and manage planning staff.

Public Information Officer: Communicate with parents and press, if appropriate. Coordinate use of mass calls or text messages. May be combined with the communications role.

Reunification Incident Commander: Coordinate Priorities, Objectives, Strategies, and Tactics for an accountable, safe reunification of students with parents.

Reunifier: Take the bottom of the Reunification Card to Assembly Area, locate the student and bring them to Reunification Area. Ask the student, "Are you okay going home with this person?" There's a lot of walking involved, so consider that when assigning people to this role.

Reunification Area Supervisor: Establish and manage the reunification area. Supervise Reunifiers.

Safety Officer: Observe site and remedy safety concerns.

Scribe: Document events. A yellow pad is sufficient.

Student Assembly Supervisor: Establish and manage the Student Assembly Area.

Supervisor: For span of control, some groups may need Supervisors.

Transportation: Direct transportation needs. May become a supervisor position.

Victim Advocate/Mental Health Professional: Standby unless needed.

Worker: Watch the traffic flow, and escort parents/guardians to and from the family waiting area.

ON-SITE PARTIAL REUNIFICATION
Incident Command Structure

This chart is an example of the organizational structure that might be used to conduct an On-site Partial Reunification.

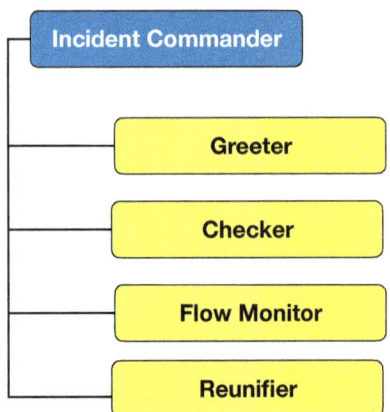

Partial reunification is conducted when only part of the student body will need to be reunited, and very often results from a school being in Secure Protocol. It may be needed at the conclusion of a school day when there is an ongoing hazardous condition outside the school or in the area. It may be due to criminal activity in the area or a local hazard that makes it unsafe for the students who usually walk home to do so.

Students who ride the bus home would still do so. If there is criminal activity in the area, the bus loading area will require elevated situational awareness and extra staff.

In some rural communities this might only involve a few students, whereas in many urban schools it might be majority of the student population, in which case the number of roles as described on page 15 would be expanded.

Schools and districts should conduct a tabletop exercise in advance to talk through the potential hazards and discuss how to manage them.

Student Drivers

The age of the students will play a big role in how the school handles this. High school-age students will be able to manage much more independently than the younger students. Make a plan to address those who drive to and from school, and any students who carpool with them.

Workflow

A partial reunification can typically be successfully completed quickly with the school staff. However, there may be increased law enforcement nearby, and they may be available to assist. The minimum number of recommended roles is five people, plus one per 100 students to conduct this.

Students may either stay in a room with their teacher or be brought to an assembly area. In the assembly area, students remain with their teacher and classmates to maintain accountability. Discuss this in advance to decide what works best for your school.

We recommend parents and guardians show identification when they arrive at a check-in location. This ensures the correct person is picking up the student. Additionally, it displays an organized, thought-out process that will help maintain order and control in a potentially uncertain situation.

It's not uncommon to have a few students left if all parents cannot be located. It is the schools' and districts' responsibility to plan for this.

Communication

Notification of danger outside the school is usually received by the school from local public safety partners. If this is the case, keep lines of communication open throughout the duration of the incident to monitor events. If the situation is not resolved or minimized by the normal release time, students may be held until it's safe enough to release the buses and for parents to pick up the students who normally walk home.

Contact parents as soon as the problem is identified to let them know the students are safe inside, and the day will proceed as usual, except that activities normally held outdoors will be held indoors. Set expectations as clearly as possible to keep stress levels down. This includes telling students what is happening and why you're using the Secure action.

If there is ongoing criminal activity in the area, parents and volunteers are discouraged from coming to the school, as that would put them in harm's way. If the situation becomes more manageable, the school might allow for monitored entry and controlled release. Communicate this to parents. There will be instances when a parent has arranged to pick up their child for an appointment during the day. Depending on what's going on and the information available, the school will have to decide how to handle that.

ON-SITE FULL REUNIFICATION

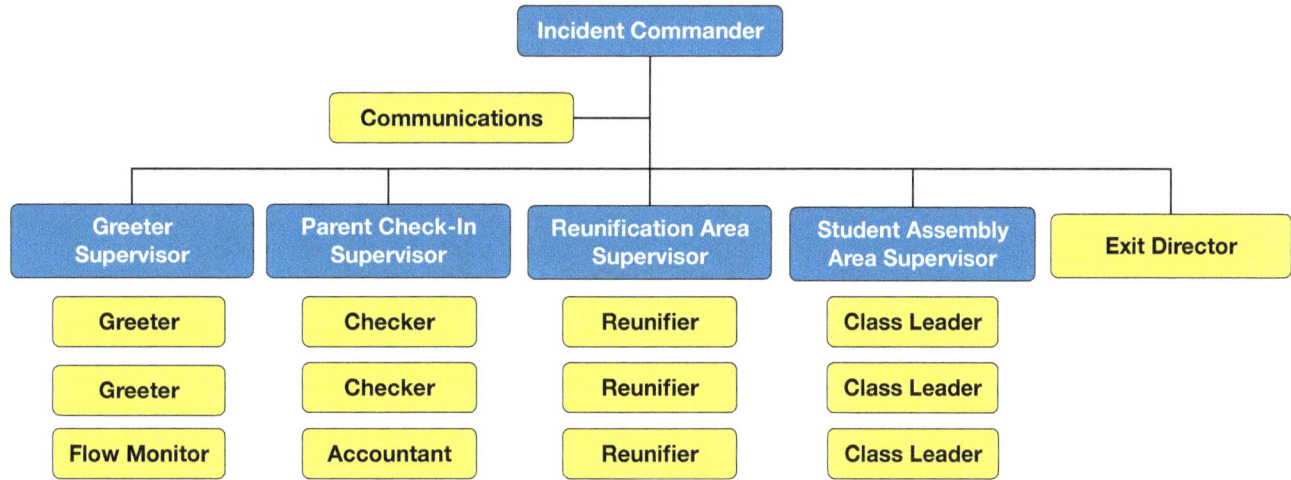

Incident Command Structure

The chart above is an example of the organizational structure that might be used to conduct an On-site Full Reunification. Remember, the minimum recommendation is five people, plus one per 100 students. The additional personnel per 100 students will typically fill more checker, greeter, reunifier, or flow monitor roles as needed. If available, the exit director role can also be filled.

This shows the Incident Commander, a Communications person, and all of the Operations Section roles. In this example, the Incident Commander oversees the Operations Section directly. There is no Planning, Finance, or Logistics section. If these roles became necessary, the Incident Commander could assign them as needed.

An on-site reunification is for an event such as a power outage, or water system or mechanical failure, which disrupts school operations. The event is small enough that the school isn't in danger but significant enough that it's not safe to continue operations for the remainder of the school day, and students will leave at an unusual time.

Sending students home on buses may not be a good plan because they could be arriving at locked and empty houses.

As with partial reunification, be sure to develop a plan for students who drive and those who ride with them.

Workflow

A full on-site reunification can often be completed by school staff, but they may request assistance from the District. Again, students may either stay in a room with their teacher or be brought to an assembly area. In the assembly area, students remain with their teacher and classmates to maintain accountability. Discuss this in advance to decide what works best for your school.

Utilize the same parent/guardian identification method recommended for partial on-site reunification. Nothing changes in the process between the two types of reunifications, but it does expand with more support staff and more students to reunite.

Communication

Parent/guardian notification for an on-site reunification can most often be handled by the affected school staff. If needed, district personnel should be available to support.

Once it is determined that an unplanned dismissal will be occurring, the school initiates the preplanned communication protocol. Typically this involves phone calls, email, and text messages to parents and guardians. Inform them of the issue and why the change in dismissal time is occurring. It is important to inform them of the reason to avoid any unnecessary confusion or panic.

Even though the incident may not seem like a big event, be prepared for the media to arrive. Often times a story involving a school will fit nicely in the day's news cycle. Ensure staff is properly trained and briefed on what to say. Things like "we were well trained to conduct the reunification and are following our plan" will sound much better than "we were caught off guard but we are figuring it out." Having a well thought-out and practiced plan will make everyone more at ease, and that mindset will show during any media coverage.

OFF-SITE REUNIFICATION OVERVIEW

During an off-site reunification, as described on the following pages, there will be two separate teams. The district reunification team will deploy to the reunification site while a second team will go to the impacted school. This second team will facilitate transportation and initiate accountability processing. They are responsible for the safe evacuation and transportation of students, teachers, and staff to the reunification site, whether it's a walking or driving location.

During a non-traumatic event, school staff may be able to serve as the impacted site team. After a traumatic event, however, they may not be able to fill those roles so it's recommended that the district sets up and trains the two-team method. Law enforcement should also be included in this training, as district teams may not be able to get to the scene and it is imperative that accountability and transportation occur in an orderly and normalized process.

> **NASP Online:**
> **Reunification Following School Evacuation**
>
> Ideally, the reunification site should be within walking distance so that the school is not dependent on other means of transportation, as arranging for buses in the immediate aftermath of a crisis or disaster that requires evacuation can be very challenging. However, in some situations, it may be best to evacuate students further away from the site; thus, coordination must occur with district and/or community transportation personnel to plan for the use of district transportation in emergency situations. Transportation to and from the reunification site must include explicit consideration of students with disabilities and special needs. For some of these students, an individual evacuation plan may be necessary.

TEACHERS: STAY WITH YOUR STUDENTS

Interviews with safety directors directly impacted by crisis reveal a common thread. Often teachers will group together in the immediate aftermath, or assume their job is done when the police arrive on the scene. It's important to emphasize that teachers remain with their students and aren't done until all of the students have been reunited with their families.

If possible, have teachers fill the roles of class leaders. This will assist with accountability as the teachers can remain with their students throughout the evacuation and reunification process. If the teachers are unable to fill that role, a pool of additional staff, such as teaching assistants, should be ready to step in. Teachers may be unable for a variety of reasons. They themselves could be parents and need to retrieve their own children. Additionally, the stress of an evacuation and reunification may impact their abilities to fill the role.

Be sure to include teachers in the process and training. Inform them of counseling resources beforehand and have mental health professionals available as a part of your reunification team.

IMPACTED SCHOOL: TRANSPORT TEAM

The team at the impacted school has these priorities:

- Assemble a master student roster, teacher roster, and guest roster;
- Identify and notify the reunification site;
- Provide safe transport of students and staff to the reunification site;
- Assign District personnel to go to the receiving health facilities if there are injuries, in coordination with Incident Command.

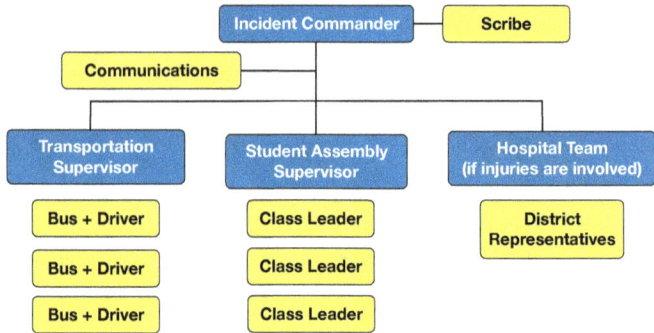

TRANSPORT ROLES AND DUTIES

The following outlines the roles and duties of the Transportation Unit. For detailed tasks, see the Job Action Sheets.

Transportation Supervisor: Whether the district runs its own buses or the service is contracted out, the Transportation Supervisor should be involved in all planning, drilling, and training for reunification.

In combination with the Student Assembly Supervisor, coordinate resources (people and vehicles) to execute the safe and accountable movement of students and staff from an impacted site to the reunification site, whether it's a walking or driving location.

Supervise an orderly movement of people from the impacted site to the reunification site, and maintain communication with the reunification site about arrivals. Depending on the incident, you may want to keep the bus loading area secure and as uncrowded as possible. After a violent incident, securing the bus loading area will most likely be managed by Law Enforcement personnel.

Class Leaders at the Impacted Site: Report to the Student Assembly Supervisor. Communicate via radio to get students to the transportation area. Most often the Class Leader role is filled by teachers who will remain with the class during evacuation and at the reunification site to maintain accountability and continuity.

Scribe: Document the events. This includes all activities, updates, and actions and the time those took place.

UNIFIED COMMAND OVERVIEW

Unified Command is activated when there are multiple entities with legal authority to be in charge of an incident. For example, law enforcement will have authority in a school violence event, but schools and districts still remain responsible for students and staff (in loco parentis). Unified Command is sometimes used to include key incident stakeholders in decision-making and coordination. The school or district may or may not be viewed as a resource unless prior interaction and training has occurred with public safety partners.

With multiple organizations responding, Leadership of each entity with legal authority communicate with each other and channel information to the Unified Incident Commander.

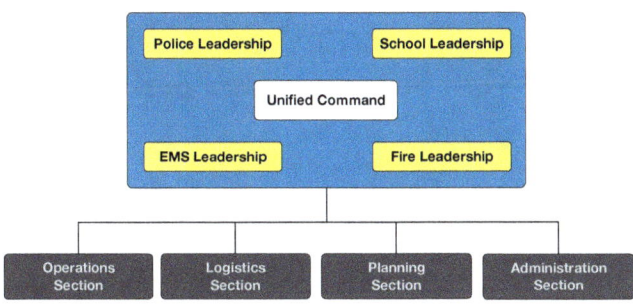

PUBLIC INFORMATION OFFICER (PIO) OR JOINT INFORMATION CENTER (JIC)?

Clear communication, both internal and external, is essential when daily routines are disrupted. Minimally, in non-violent events, external communication is handled by the school or district personnel who usually manage public messaging and social media. This person is your PIO. If the media has a presence, your PIO should be communicating with them to make sure the messaging is agreed upon and consistent.

In larger incidents, and especially when there has been violence, Unified Command is activated, and there will be a Joint Information Center. It will include Law Enforcement and/or Fire PIOs, and often an Investigator alongside the school/district PIO.

The JIC is managed by the Lead Public Information Officer (PIO). As information is obtained, the PIO brings it to Incident Command, and messaging is formulated and delivered.

INCLUDING FIRST RESPONDERS

It is absolutely imperative that as the reunification plan is developed, first responders are brought into the process. Meeting with command staff, including PIOs, both law enforcement and Fire/EMS will generate two outcomes. First, they will look at your plan from their perspective. Second, they have suggestions you might not have thought of.

In the example chart above, police, fire, EMS, and school leadership will sit together and make decisions as a single unit. The decisions will be sent out to the subordinate sections to ensure unified objectives.

LAW ENFORCEMENT SUPPORT

Depending on the type of event, the school may receive an influx of law enforcement officers. During a violent incident, the response might be overwhelming at the impacted site. Ensure that in training prior to an incident, the school, district, and law enforcement leadership is aware of additional need for law enforcement support at the reunification site.

At the reunification site, law enforcement support may be necessary. Some assignments may include:

- Traffic Control
- Crowd Control
- ID Verification
- Perimeter Control
- Security
- Liaison

LOOKING AT REUNIFICATION FROM A LAW ENFORCEMENT PERSPECTIVE

SRM V3 presents a number of organizational structures from a school or district perspective. In the face of an active assailant, when Law Enforcement takes the lead in Unified Command, they may implement an ICS structure supporting the needs of witness interviews, evidence retention, and other legal responsibilities.

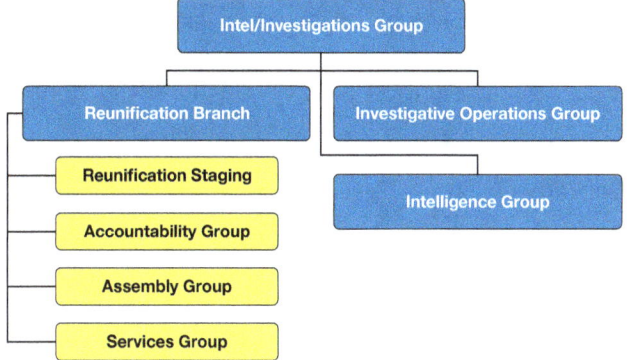

Source: C3Pathways, ASIM - https://c3.cm/asc

WHO ARE VICTIM ADVOCATES?

Many law enforcement agencies, district attorneys, and prosecutors have victim advocates on staff and a cadre of trained volunteers. In many states and counties, they are charged to protect and promote the rights of victims. They often deploy when there is a crisis. Very often they are trained in Psychological First Aid and can be helpful with crisis counseling, if needed, during a reunification. Get to know these community partners.

PARTNERSHIPS

During one Standard Reunification Method workshop conducted by The Foundation, a fire chief requested the training for every fire station in his city. When questioned why, he replied, "We are going to be on the scene. If we're not actively engaged in fire or EMS, we can help with the reunification process." This is a perfect example of a community that is ready to work as a team instead of as separate entities.

OFF-SITE REUNIFICATION - NON-VIOLENT EVENT

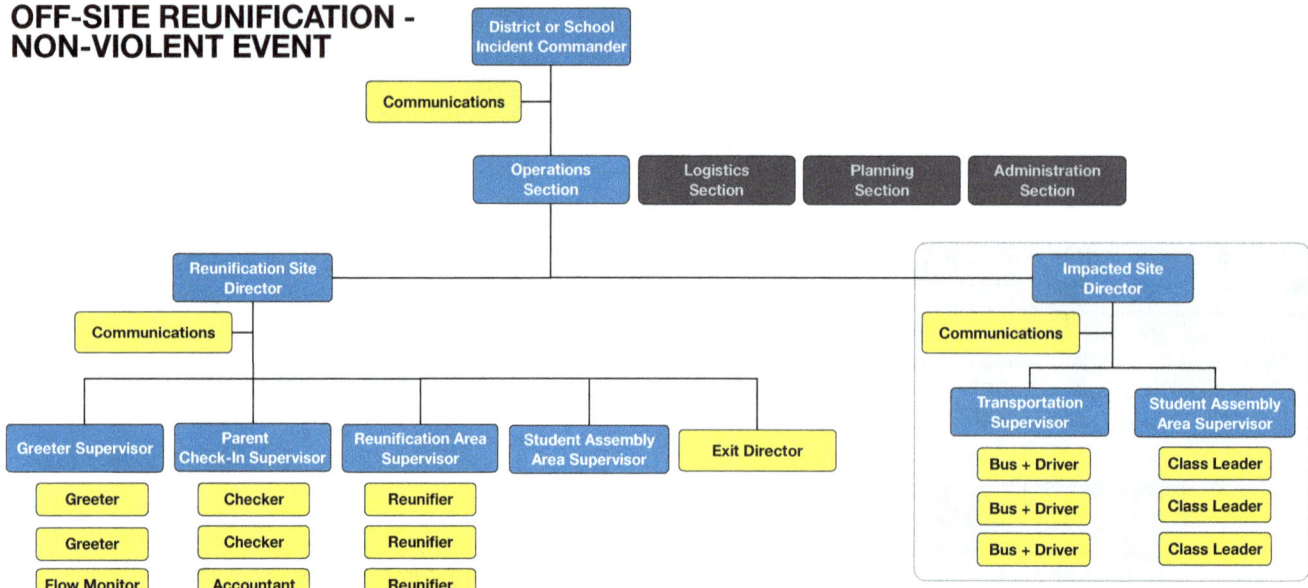

An off-site reunification is conducted when something happens that makes it unsafe or unhealthy to remain in the building, or even a specific area. This could be a gas leak, fire, potential flooding, or something similar.

Transporting students to a different location creates a very different dynamic for parents and families.

The chart above shows an example of the organizational structure that might be used to conduct an evacuation and reunification of the entire student population during a non-violent event.

Workflow

An off-site reunification requires more people simply because there are more moving parts. The minimum recommendation is five people, plus one per 100 students.

While waiting to evacuate, students may either stay in a room with their teacher or be brought to an assembly area. In the assembly area, students remain with their teacher and classmates to maintain accountability. Alternatively, you may choose to move people directly to buses, one classroom at a time.

At the reunification site, we recommend parents and guardians show identification when they arrive to pick up their child. This ensures the correct adult is picking up the student and it displays an organized, thought-out process that will help maintain order and control in a potentially chaotic situation.

It's not uncommon to have a few students left whose parents/guardians cannot make it to the site. It is the schools' and districts' responsibility to have a plan in place to address that.

Communication

Let parents know as soon as possible, and tell them exactly what is going on and when they might be able to pick up their child. If students will be transported off-site, it's advisable not to immediately tell parents where the site is, as parents may cause traffic problems before students and staff arrive.

Preparation

Create relationships in advance with other schools and community partners for reunification sites. It is advisable to create a Memorandum of Understanding with them in order to set expectations and understand responsibilities.

Plan in advance to have a site within walking distance as well as a transport site farther away. The time of day and weather conditions are some of the factors determining which site will be used.

Create classroom go-bags and have them packed with items that your student population requires.

Plan for the accommodations that your students and staff with disabilities may require, making sure to include people with temporary mobility injuries.

Have a plan in place in advance to address high school students who drive to school and/or carpool.

Law Enforcement may be available to assist with safety and traffic control.

Communication Between the Reunification Site and Impacted Site

During a non-violent event requiring evacuation and reunification, the school and district will be responsible for most of the activities. A transport team will be required at the impacted site and a reunification team will be needed at the reunification site.

The District Incident Commander could be located at the reunification site or the impacted school site. It is recommended to go to the reunification site since that location will be operating for the longer period of time.

OFF-SITE REUNIFICATION - VIOLENT EVENT
Incident Command Overview

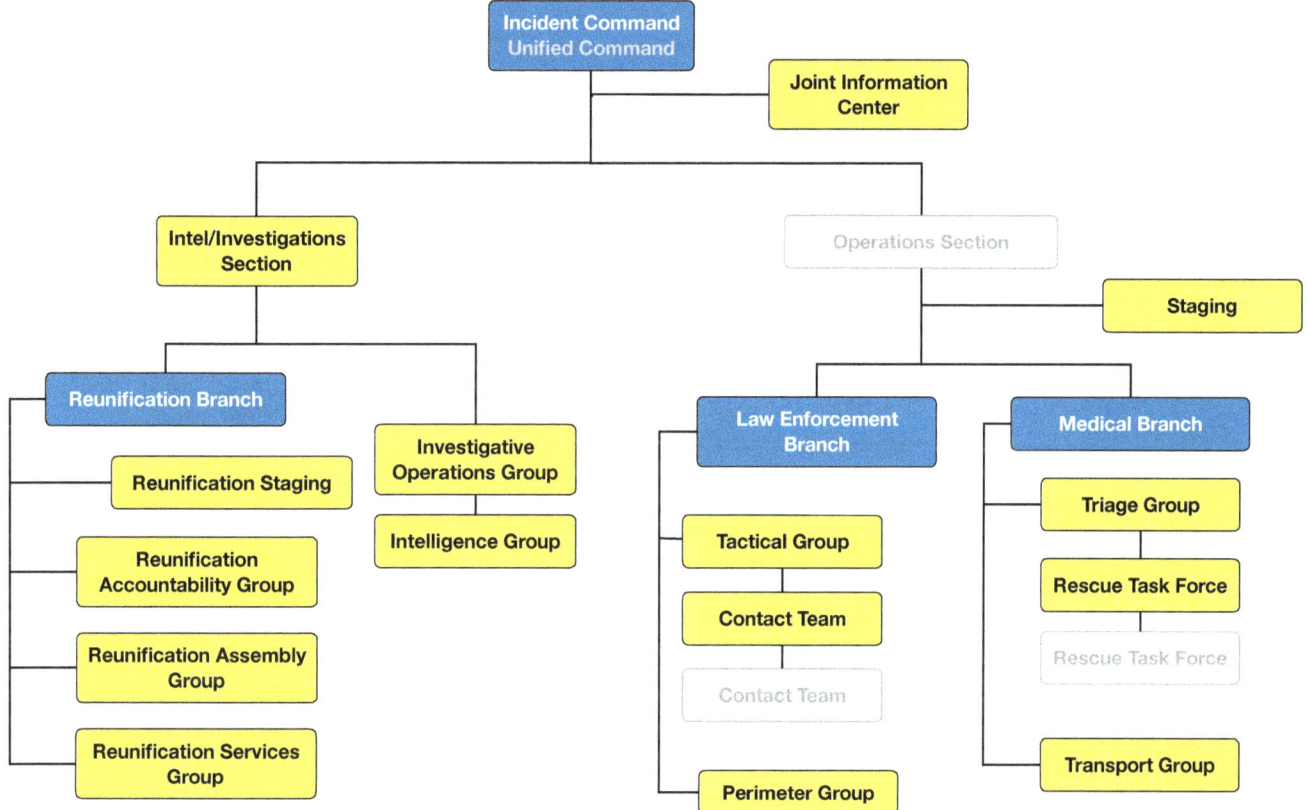

A violent event on campus dramatically changes how a reunification unfolds. Emergency responders will arrive quickly (often in just a few minutes) and begin working their priorities:

Priority 1: Neutralize the threat,

Priority 2: Rescue the injured, and

Priority 3: Clear the entire campus (i.e., verify no threats remain).

Expectations and Preparation

In a violent event, law enforcement is in charge (i.e., think attempted murder in progress). Generally, emergency responders work toward a Unified Command with affected parties as soon as practicable, but it takes time. The campus is considered not secure until Priority 3 (clearing) is completed, which – brace yourself – usually takes hours. Law enforcement will control all movement of students and staff during this period to protect them, as the campus is not secure. There is generally no movement of students or staff during Priorities 1 (neutralize the threat) and 2 (rescue the injured). Law enforcement may be delayed in connecting with and moving campus administrators to the Command Post.

Create relationships in advance with local emergency responders to learn more about their response process and procedures. Look for opportunities to deconflict policies, share information, and provide resources to speed the response (e.g., go-bags, maps, keys, etc.).

Off-Site Reunification

The campus cannot be used for reunification when a violent event occurs because it is not secure and is a crime scene. Students and staff must be moved under security from the affected site to an off-site reunification location. The off-site location must be secured by law enforcement prior to announcing the location. Transportation is obtained, the route of travel mapped, and student/parent communication is planned. Importantly, law enforcement must choreograph movement of students and staff from classrooms to a secure assembly location or directly to transportation.

Assumptions about reunification can collide with law enforcement realities when preparation is inadequate. They may be your students, but law enforcement controls everyone's movement (including other emergency responders).

Incident Command

In a violent event, Reunification becomes part of the emergency responders' existing Incident Command structure responders are using to manage the event — not a separate, stand-alone structure. This is essential to ensure coordination, information sharing, manage security, and maintain crime scene and investigative integrity. More importantly, communication mistakes can get people hurt. Plugging into the responders' Incident Command structure is the best way to ensure they know what you are doing and you know what they are doing.

Reunification Branch

The Reunification function becomes what is known as a Branch within the Incident Command System. The Reunification Branch is still a school or district led and managed function. The person in charge is called the Reunification Branch Director.

The Reunification Branch Director's "boss" is the Intel/Investigations Section Chief (law enforcement), who in turn reports to the Incident Commander or Unified Commanders (see the chart at the beginning of this section). While on the surface this may seem odd, the Intel/Investigations Section is responsible for interviewing witnesses and knowing the status and location of any injured or missing (students and staff). In a nutshell, they are the access to information, resources, and cooperation with law enforcement and other responders.

Notifications

It is beyond the scope of this document to address how injury notifications should be handled procedurally or emotionally. This is the function of the Family Assistance Center, which is part of the Reunification Services Group (alternatively, law enforcement if a Family Assistance Center is not yet established). However, it must be acknowledged that parents of injured students will arrive at the Reunification site looking for their student.

It is not acceptable for parents to wait at Reunification for hours to be told their student was injured (or is perfectly safe but delayed because law enforcement is interviewing them). Reunification staff must know the names of the injured as soon as possible so those parents can be pulled at Check-In and directed to the Family Assistance Center for help. Identifying the injured and sharing the information quickly is not an easy task, but it is possible when everyone works together. It is easier if schools train and practice with responders ahead of time.

Workflow from Lockdown to Reunification

The detail in this section is to educate school personnel about what is happening while they're in lockdown during a violent event — and why it takes so long.

A violent event should trigger a campus lockdown and 911 activation. Law enforcement will arrive quickly and move directly to the threat (or last known location) to neutralize the threat. They will assume the entire campus is a danger zone (unsecure), moving through hallways quickly with their weapons at the ready, including possibly carrying long guns. This may continue even after a threat is neutralized. As additional law enforcement and fire/EMS responders arrive, they will begin working to rescue and transport the injured. There is typically no movement of students or staff during this period, except for those being rescued.

While a known threat is typically neutralized in 10 minutes or less (90% of the time), the rescue and transport of injured may take an additional 20-30 minutes. Students and staff should have an expectation of being in lockdown for 45-60 minutes with little or no information.

As law enforcement moves into the clearing phase (Priority 3), informational updates should begin. District personnel may already be at the Command Post. If a campus administrator is not at the Command Post, law enforcement will typically prioritize locating and moving an administrator. Unified Command should be initiated if it's not already established.

There are literally hundreds of decisions and actions that must occur in collaboration with an extensive team (e.g., law enforcement, fire/EMS, school, emergency management, etc.). If possible, use the school's public address system to update students and staff with simple messages of reassurance and desired action. Information to those in lockdown can lessen fear and emotional trauma immensely.

Considerations

It takes time — a lot of time. There are things to know and things to do.

- Disseminate information to students, staff, and the public as soon as practicable. The Lead PIO must get messaging approval from the Incident Commander/Unified Commanders. Sometimes law enforcement holds back information to protect the investigation or maintain security.
- Every classroom must be cleared. Law enforcement should plan to conduct emotionally responsible room entries when clearing the rooms to avoid further traumatizing students and staff.
- In most cases, every student and staff member will be patted down (searched) for weapons. It is preferable to conduct this out of the public's sight.
- Students and staff should be kept away from the site of the violence and damage while they're being moved through the building and out of the school.
- Law enforcement MUST secure the reunification site before its location information is leaked (and it quickly will be). If more than one reunification site is being considered, secure them all until a decision is made.

OFF-SITE REUNIFICATION - VIOLENT EVENT
School/District Responsibilities Overview

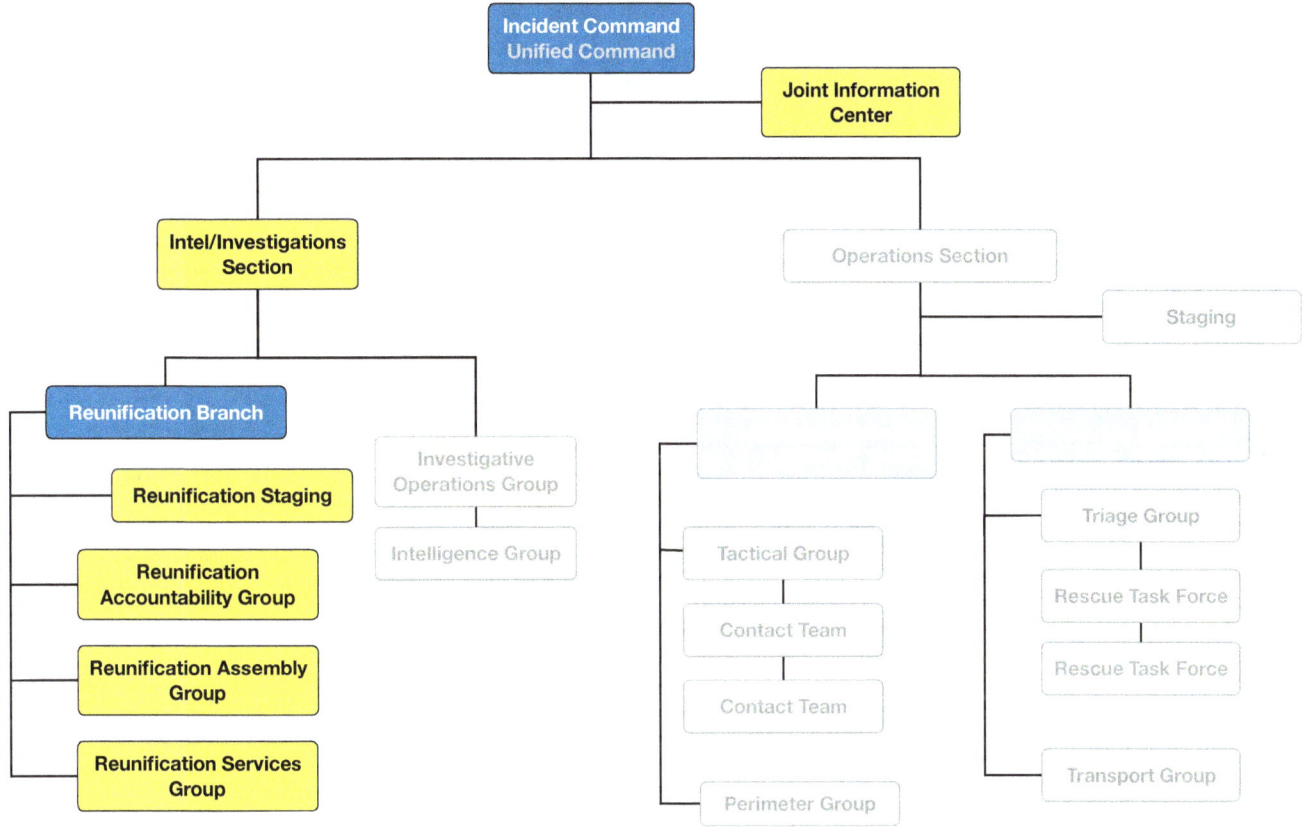

- Be aware responders will want to announce the reunification site as soon as possible to keep parents away from the scene, whereas district personnel may desire to wait until students are moved (this can be a point of conflict).
- Determine the names of those transported to hospitals and any fatalities. The Family Assistance Center (part of the Services Group) should work with EMS and law enforcement to make this a priority so parent/guardian notifications are made timely.
- Have paper backup available for electronic systems. It is common for wi-fi and cellular networks to become congested and fail from the volume of traffic. Have remote (or secondary) access for electronic systems (e.g., video surveillance, attendance records, public address, two-way radios, etc.). If the violent event occurs in the office area, it will not be possible to enter and use systems in that location, as it's a crime scene.
- Pre-assemble "Go Bags" for responders that are equipped with master keys and maps to the entire campus — preferably color-coded keys and maps. This not only speeds response, but it can prevent hundreds of thousands of dollars damage from responders breaching doors and locks. A locked door will not stop responders; it works out better for everyone if they have keys.

NOTE: Law enforcement responders may not have access to Knox Boxes required by some fire departments.

Practice with Emergency Responders

Success requires practice, and not practice in isolation. Practice with your local emergency responders. Build relationships. Get to know your City or County's Emergency Manager. Know what to expect from each other. And remember PPE (Personalities, Politics, and Egos) can cost lives, so leave it at the door.

SRP Lifecycle with

EXAMPLE 1: SECURE

Scenario: Criminal activity in the area has resulted in the school going into the Secure protocol. Students were brought into the building. Business as usual inside, but no one is let in or out.

Law enforcement has indicated that school can be released at the normal time, even though the situation outside isn't completely resolved.

Considerations: With criminal activity in area of the school, it's decided that students who walk home should have their parents/guardians pick them up.

Incident Command: Because there was no criminal or safety issue in the school, Incident Command would be led by the school safety team. Coordination with Law Enforcement Incident Command about the status of the criminal activity would be necessary.

Public Information Officer: Because the school was not directly involved in criminal activity, the school or district would lead public information within the school community. The District and Law Enforcement PIOs work with the Incident Commander to develop media messaging.

Notifications: Depending on the situation, parents/guardians and media will be notified of what is occurring and the status of student reunification. Additional notification will be made to parents who would need to pick up their students.

Police Role in Reunification: With criminal activity in the area, but not directly near the school, officers may be asked to assist with reunification. Some duties might include assisting with parent/guardian identification (for the parents without ID), traffic control, or simply uniformed presence. Patrol resources may also be relocated near the school.

SECURE LIFECYCLE
- School is placed in Secure Protocol.
- Parents/guardians are notified.
- Business goes on as usual within the school as much as possible.
- Law enforcement presence around the school may be increased.
- At release time, if the situation hasn't been resolved, the Standard Reunification Method is utilized for the students who walk home at the end of school day.

EXAMPLE 2: LOCKDOWN

Scenario: An armed intruder is seen in the school building by a staff member who announces a Lockdown and calls 911. Students and staff immediately take action to avoid injury. The intruder causes damage to the building prior to Law Enforcement arriving.

Considerations: Because it is an active law enforcement response and investigation, the decision is made to transport students to a nearby community center for reunification.

Unified Command: Because it is an active crime scene, law enforcement would establish a unified command with school officials.

Reunification Incident Command: At the reunification site, a command structure is established to manage the reunification.

Joint Information Center: Because it is an active crime scene, the law enforcement PIO would be the primary press representative. The school or district PIO would be in the JIC, communicating with the PIO at the reunification site.

Notifications: Parents/guardians and media are notified that the school has been placed in Lockdown. Additional notifications are made to parents/guardians about the location of the reunification site once students are in route or at the site.

Police Role in Reunification: While the school has become an active crime scene, some officers will be assigned to the reunification site. Depending on the site, police may decide to sweep the area prior to students arriving. In addition to the duties outlined in the Secure example, detectives may be on scene for witness interviews and statements.

LOCKDOWN LIFECYCLE
- School is placed in Lockdown Protocol.
- Multiple law enforcement agencies arrive on scene.
- Parents/guardians begin to arrive outside of the police perimeter.
- Media arrives on scene.
- Internet, WiFi, and cell services become intermittent or unresponsive.
- Police secure the reunification site.
- District mobilizes Reunification Team.
- Buses are deployed and students are transported to the reunification site.
- Parents/guardians are notified of location.
- The Standard Reunification Method is utilized.

Reunification

EXAMPLE 3: EVACUATE
Scenario: An unknown cause has resulted in thick smoke in a school. Students successfully evacuate to the football field.

Considerations: Because it is still an active fire response and investigation and the area is experiencing inclement weather, a decision is made to transport students to a nearby high school for reunification.

Unified Command: Because it is an active fire event, the fire department would establish unified command with school officials.

Reunification Incident Command: At the reunification site, a command structure is established to manage the reunification.

Joint Information Center: Because it is an active fire event, the fire department PIO would be the primary press representative. The school or district PIO would be in the JIC, communicating with the PIO at the reunification site.

Notifications: Parents/guardians and media are notified that the school has been evacuated. Additional notifications are made to parents/guardians about the location of the reunification site once students are in route or at the site.

Police Role in Reunification: While the school is an active fire scene, the school requests assistance from law enforcement. Officers are assigned to the reunification site.

EVACUATE LIFECYCLE
- Parents/guardians begin to arrive outside the perimeter.
- The media arrive on scene.
- Internet, WiFi, and cell services are intermittent or unresponsive.
- Police secure the reunification site.
- District mobilizes Reunification Team.
- Buses are deployed and students are transported to the reunification site.
- Parents/guardians are notified of site location.
- The Standard Reunification Method is utilized.

EXAMPLE 4: SHELTER
Scenario: A tornado has unexpectedly touched down in a neighborhood. The local elementary school has gone into the Shelter Protocol with all students and staff taking refuge in appropriate locations.

Considerations: The tornado blew down trees and power lines. Roads are closed and there is no access to the school at this time. The school was not damaged, but students will need to remain on-site until the roads are cleared and their parents/guardians can arrive.

Unified Command: School officials will be working with the district, local emergency management, law enforcement, public works, and utility companies to clear the roads and get access to the school.

Reunification Incident Command: The school is serving as the reunification site. Since the school was not damaged, there was no need for an evacuation. The school staff will serve as the reunification team.

Joint Information Center: The district PIO will work with the town officials to handle communications and notifications.

Notifications: Parents and media are notified that the school was undamaged and all students and staff are safe at this time. Parents will be notified once the roads are cleared and they can pick up their children.

Police Role in Reunification: Law Enforcement will be used to ensure the safety of the tree clearance teams. They may be requested to help with traffic flow in and around the school once the roads are clear.

SHELTER LIFECYCLE
- Shelter Protocol is enacted, students and staff take shelter.
- Shelter is lifted once it is safe.
- Notification goes out to parents.
- School ensures the safety of the students, and prepares for a reunification.
- Routes are cleared.
- Parents begin to arrive.
- The Standard Reunification Method is utilized.

SRM Staging the

STEP 1
ESTABLISH ON-SITE INCIDENT COMMAND
The first step in staging for transport is establishing School Incident Command at the affected school. Integrating with Unified Command should be a priority.

Priorities: Student and staff safety and wellbeing; Student and staff whereabouts and condition; Assemble affected school command staff; Integrate with Unified Command; Establish Joint Information Center.
Objectives: Safe transport of students and staff to reunification site.
Strategy: The Standard Reunification Method.
Tactics: Will be determined by the environment.

STEP 2
CLASSROOM EVACUATION
Classrooms are individually evacuated to the Secure Assembly Area. During a Police-Led Evacuation, students and staff will be asked to keep their hands visible.

If it is a Police-Led Evacuation after a Lockdown, each room will be cleared by Law Enforcement personnel. This process may take up to several hours. Teacher should take attendance in the classroom prior to evacuation.

SPECIAL NEEDS POPULATIONS
The Individuals with Disabilities Act mandates additional supports for students with special education needs in school setting. These supports would also function to provide supervision and assistance to students with disabilities during emergency situations.

SRM Actions and

COMMUNITY ACTION
PARENTS WILL BEGIN TO ARRIVE
Parents will be arriving at the impacted school. Often with a Lockdown event, adjoining schools will go into Lockout. Parents may be arriving at those schools as well.

REUNIFICATION SITE
MOBILIZE REUNIFICATION TEAM
Contacting the Superintendent and determining the Reunification Site are among the first actions taken. If the site is another school, early release may be necessary.

School for Transport

STEP 3
SECURE ASSEMBLY AREA
At the Secure Assembly Area, it is preferable that teachers stay with their students. If some teachers are unable to be at the Secure Assembly Area, doubling up classes with "Partner" teachers is appropriate.

STEP 4
STUDENT AND STAFF TRANSPORT
Students and staff board the bus and are transported to the Reunification Site. Buses having audio video systems can be utilized for further accountability by having students face the camera and state their name.

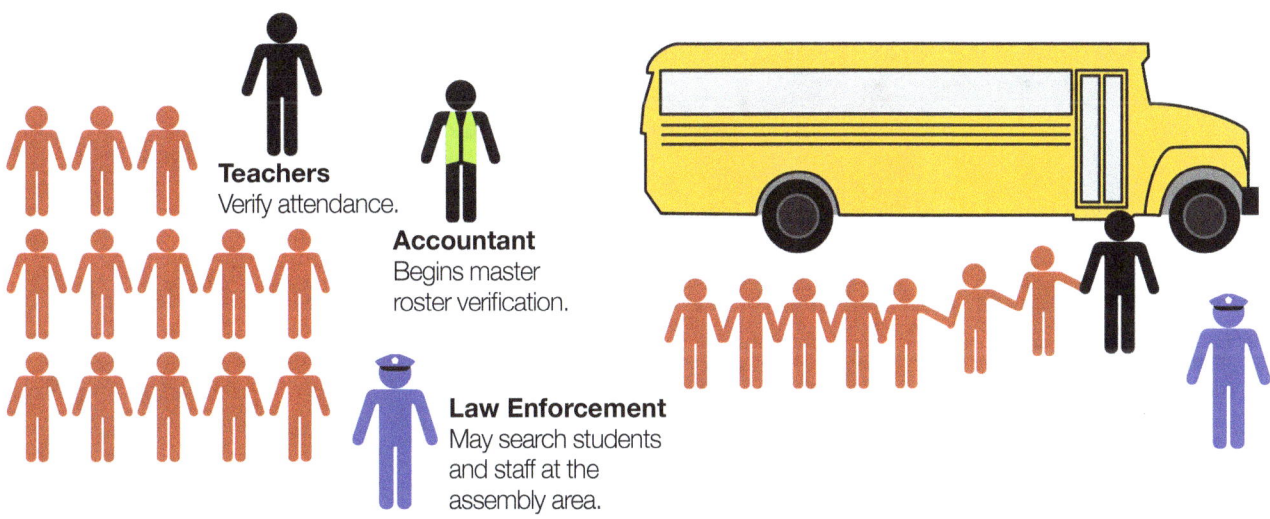

Teachers Verify attendance.

Accountant Begins master roster verification.

Law Enforcement May search students and staff at the assembly area.

Considerations

LAW ENFORCEMENT
SUPPORT AND INVESTIGATIONS
Regardless of criminal activity, law enforcement support will be necessary at both the impacted school and the reunification site.

FIRE AND EMS
CASUALTY CARE
If necessary, Fire and EMS will establish Casualty Collection, Triage and Transport areas. Many fire departments are also willing to assist in the transport and reunification process, if they are not actively responding to crisis.

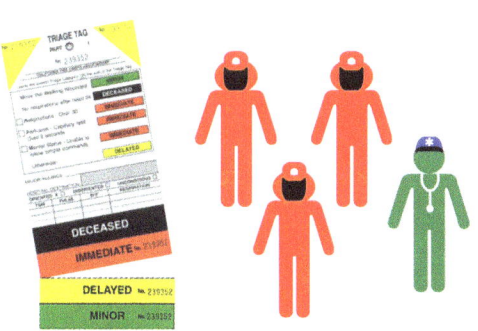

SRM Staging the

ASSEMBLY AREA
STUDENTS ENTER OUT OF PARENTAL VIEW

Students are transported to the Reunification Site and are then directed to the Student Assembly Area. Often this is a cafeteria or gymnasium. Upon arrival, students are verified against a master roster.

It is important that students are not in view of their parents when exiting the bus and entering the reunification site.

GREETING AREA
PARENTS ARE MET HERE

As parents arrive, signage directs them to Parent Check-in Table. Greeters begin the process by asking parents to complete the Reunification Card.

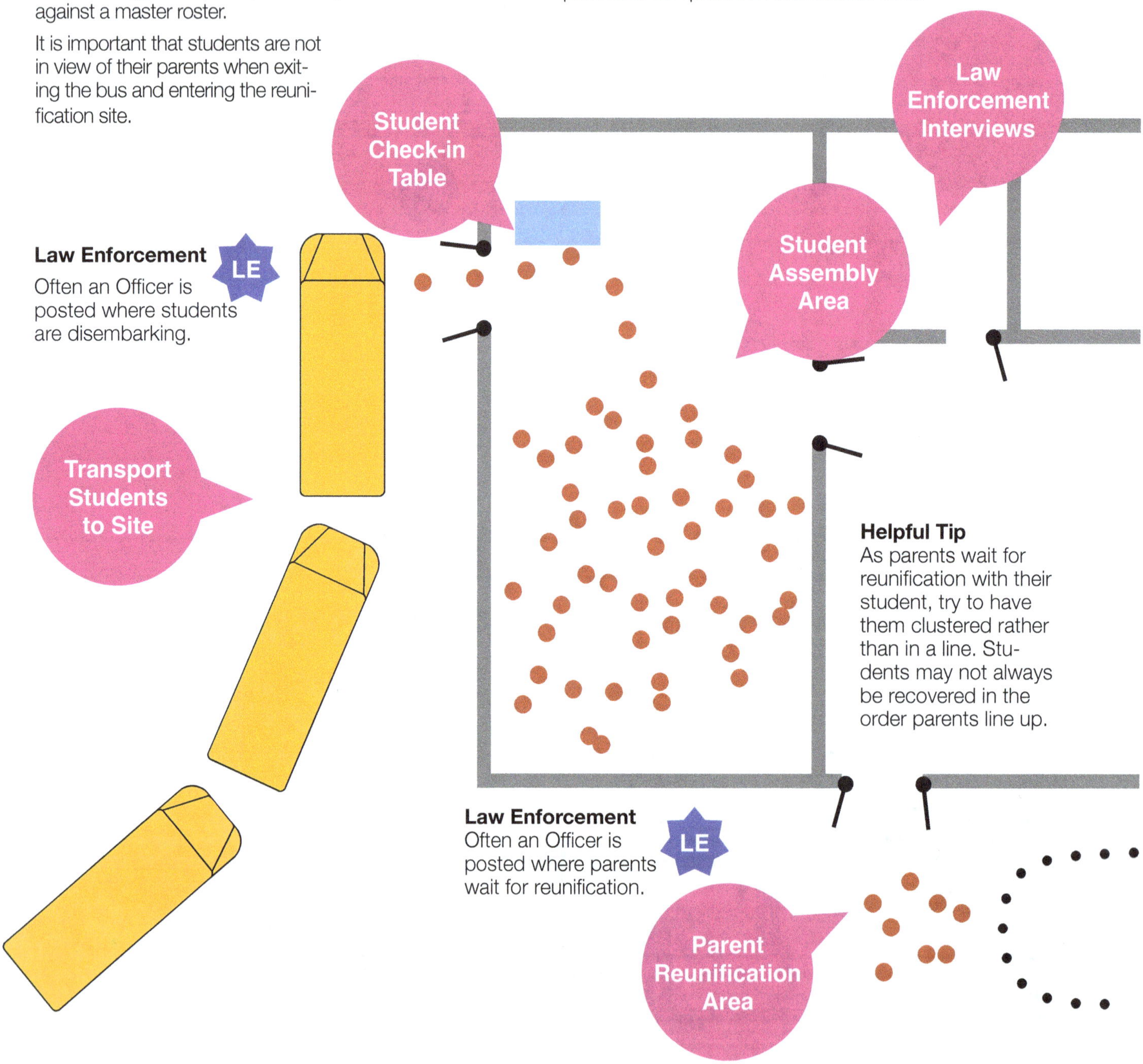

Law Enforcement
Often an Officer is posted where students are disembarking.

Transport Students to Site

Student Check-in Table

Law Enforcement Interviews

Student Assembly Area

Helpful Tip
As parents wait for reunification with their student, try to have them clustered rather than in a line. Students may not always be recovered in the order parents line up.

Law Enforcement
Often an Officer is posted where parents wait for reunification.

Parent Reunification Area

Reunification Site

CHECK-IN TABLE
SET UP MULTIPLE LINES
Establish parallel check-in lines based on first initial of last name. Checkers verify ID and custody.

REUNIFICATION AREA
PARENT STUDENT REUNIFICATION
As their tasks are completed, Greeters and Checkers can be reassigned as Reunifiers.

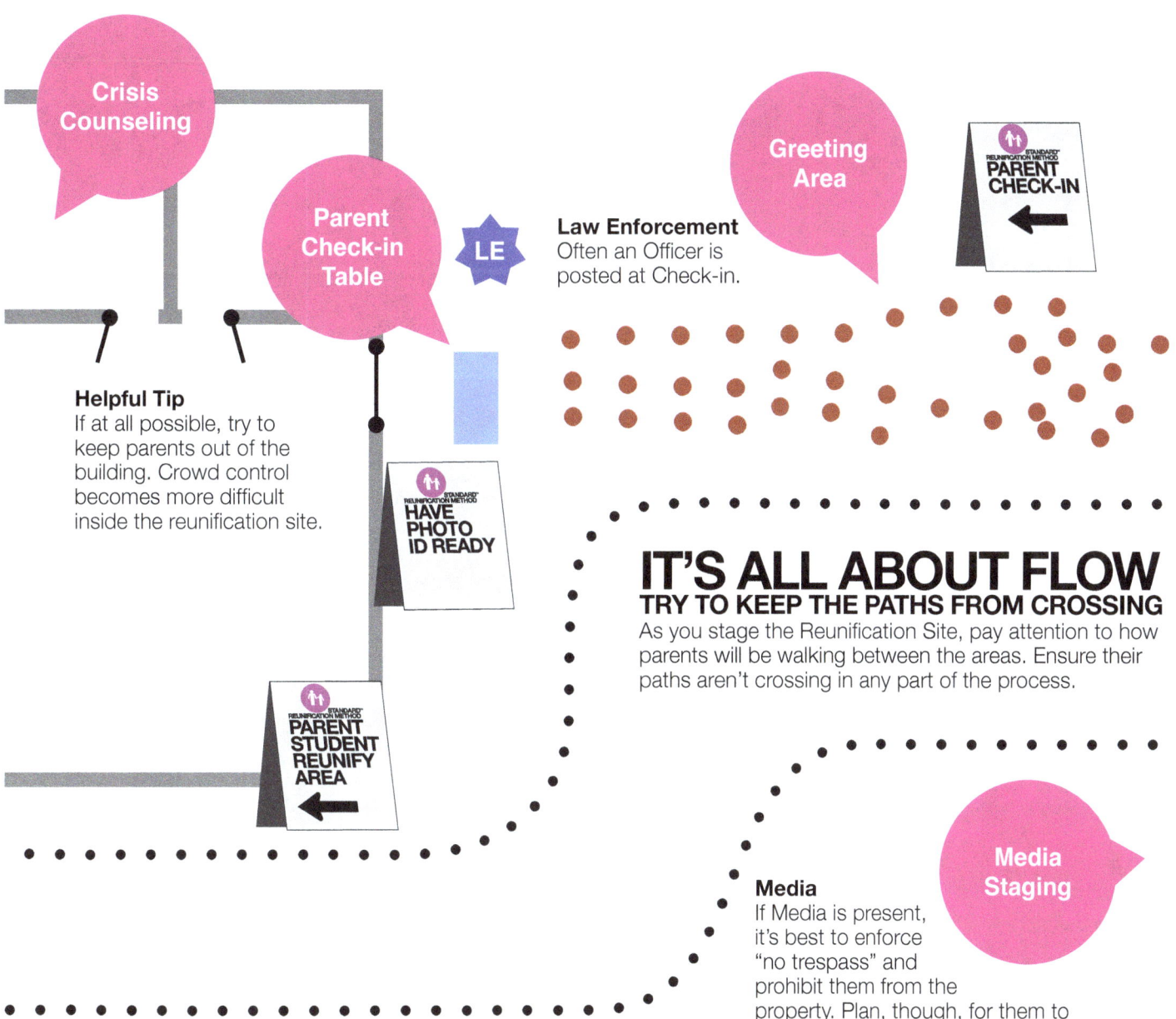

Crisis Counseling

Parent Check-in Table

LE

Greeting Area

Law Enforcement
Often an Officer is posted at Check-in.

Helpful Tip
If at all possible, try to keep parents out of the building. Crowd control becomes more difficult inside the reunification site.

IT'S ALL ABOUT FLOW
TRY TO KEEP THE PATHS FROM CROSSING
As you stage the Reunification Site, pay attention to how parents will be walking between the areas. Ensure their paths aren't crossing in any part of the process.

Media
If Media is present, it's best to enforce "no trespass" and prohibit them from the property. Plan, though, for them to be parked across the street.

Media Staging

SRM The Process

Step 1
Greetings

As parents arrive at the reunification site, Greeters explain the process and distribute Reunification Cards.

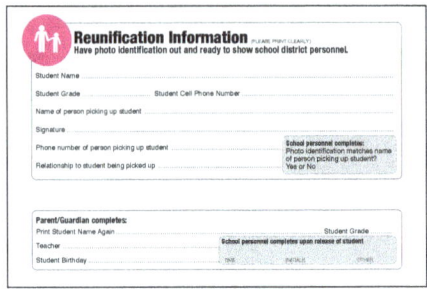

Step 2
Parents fill out card

Parents complete the information requested on the card and begin to self sort into lines.

Step 3
Checkers Verify ID

Parent custody is verified using established district procedures. The card is torn on the perforation. The bottom is returned to the parent, and the top is given to the Accountant.

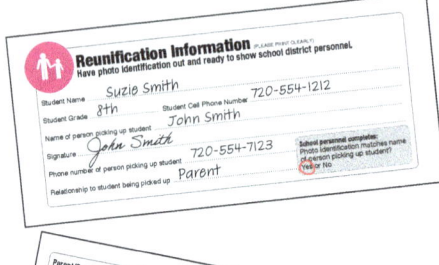

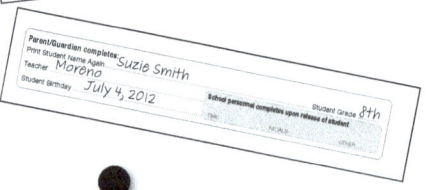

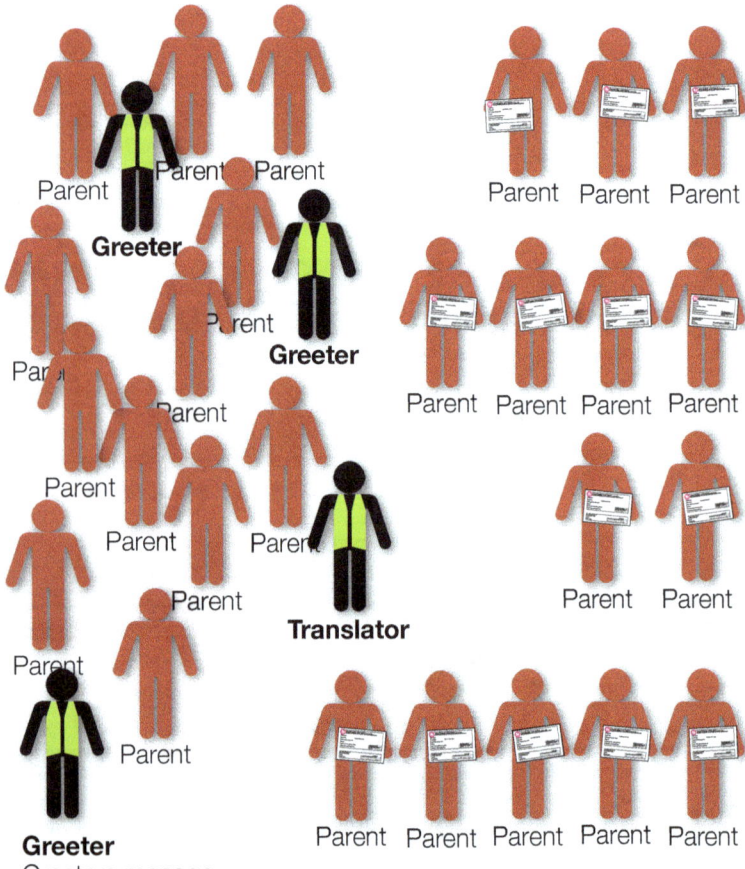

Greeter
Greeters manage the initial intake of parents. They explain the process and answer questions that may arise.

Accountant
The Accountant verifies cards against a master roster and may start sorting cards.

Law Enforcement
A uniformed officer can help with crowd control and identity verification.

Checker
Checkers verify identification. In some cases custodial authority may need verification as well.

in 6 easy steps

Step 4
Reunification Area
At the Reunification Area, parents give the bottom of the card to a Reunifier. The Reunifier goes to the Assembly area to recover the student.

Step 5
Student Reunification
The Reunifier returns the student to their parents asking the student if they feel comfortable leaving with that adult. They then note the time and initial the bottom of the card.

Step 6
Accountability
The Reunifier delivers the bottom of the card to the Exit Accountant. The Accountant may start sorting the cards.

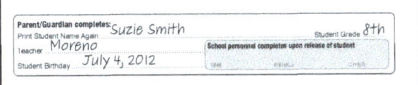
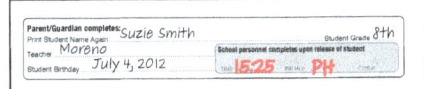

Parent Parent Parent **Reunifier**

Reunifier Parent

Reunifier Accountant

Principal
It may be beneficial to have the school principal in the area where students and parents are reunited.

What If?
the student isn't there?
If the student isn't in the Assembly Area, the Reunifier hands the card to a Victim Advocate/Crisis Counselor.

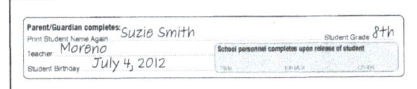

Separate
the parent from the line.
The Victim Advocate/Crisis Counselor then separates the parent from the other parents in line and brings them to a private location.

Reunifier **Counselor**

Counselor

Parent Parent Parent Parent

Law Enforcement
A uniformed officer can help with crowd control and keep the peace.

SRM The Card

REUNIFICATION INFORMATION CARDS

The Standard Reunification Method was created to manage not just the students, but the parental experience of reunification as well. The Reunification Card is an essential element of the method.

Some might initially protest, "What! More Paperwork?" And the answer is "Yes. Precisely." Beyond providing a mechanism for accountability, the card demonstrates to parents that there is a process for this. It shows that school or district has a plan and a method.

The psychology behind the process begins to offer the parent some measure of order in what might be a stressful time. Filling the card out, then separating the top from the bottom, handing the card to the Reunifier, gives the parent feedback, demonstrating progress in the process. The bottom of the card also provides proxy identification for the parent, removing the need to ID them at every phase.

Send it home in advance?

A question often comes up about whether the school should send the cards home in advance and request parents fill out and return them. Certainly an option, but it creates unnecessary work in collecting the cards, and diminishes the parent experience. One alternative is to send the cards home with the handout, and ask parents to complete the card and put it in their car. This gives parents an expectation of the process and some parents will complete the request.

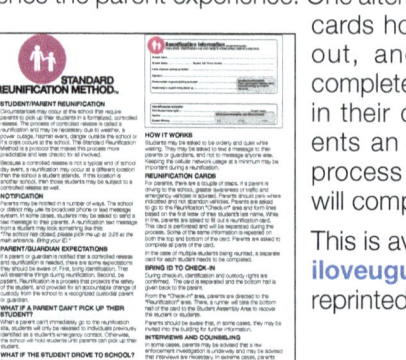

This is available at iloveuguys.org and is also reprinted on page 34.

AVAILABLE IN SPANISH

The Reunification Card is also available in Spanish. Check the website for new translations.

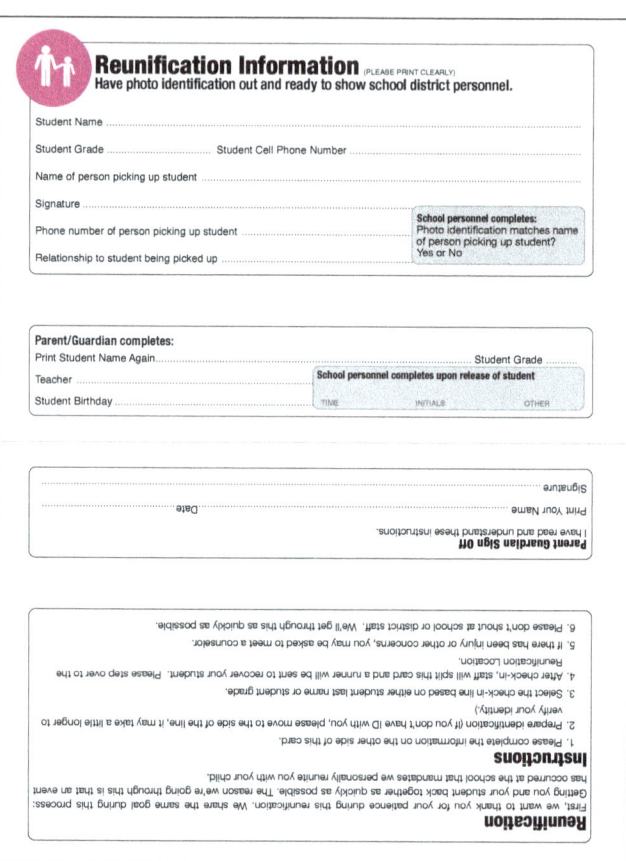

PRESS READY ARTWORK

The Reunification Cards are press ready for your printer. The artwork is set up for Work and Tumble [1] on 8½" x 11" index card stock. Ask your printer for a strong perforation. There is little worse than a "bad perf" on reunification day.

[1] "In pre-press and printing, an imposition or layout in which one plate contains all the images (pages) to be printed on both sides of a sheet. When one side of a job has been printed, the pile of printed sheets is turned over, the edge of the sheet that was the gripper edge for the first side becoming the back edge for the second side. After printing, the sheet is cut in half, yielding two identical units."

Source: PrintWiki – the Free Encyclopedia of Print. http://printwiki.org

Reunification Information (PLEASE PRINT CLEARLY)
Have photo identification out and ready to show school district personnel.

Student Name ....

Student Grade .... Student Cell Phone Number ....

Name of person picking up student ....

Signature ....

Phone number of person picking up student ....

Relationship to student being picked up ....

School personnel completes:
Photo identification matches name of person picking up student?
Yes or No

Parent/Guardian completes:

Print Student Name Again.. Student Grade ....

Teacher ....

Student Birthday ....

School personnel completes upon release of student

TIME   INITIALS   OTHER

Reunification

First, we want to thank you for your patience during this reunification. We share the same goal during this process: Getting you and your student back together as quickly as possible. The reason we're going through this is that an event has occurred at the school that mandates we personally reunite you with your child.

Instructions

1. Please complete the information on the other side of this card.
2. Prepare identification (if you don't have ID with you, please move to the side of the line, it may take a little longer to verify your identity.)
3. Select the check-in line based on either student last name or student grade.
4. After check-in, staff will split this card and a runner will be sent to recover your student. Please step over to the Reunification Location.
5. If there has been injury or other concerns, you may be asked to meet a counselor.
6. Please don't shout at school or district staff. We'll get through this as quickly as possible.

Parent Guardian Sign Off
I have read and understand these instructions.

Print Your Name .... Date ....

Signature ....

STANDARD REUNIFICATION METHOD™

STUDENT/PARENT REUNIFICATION

Circumstances may occur at the school that require parents to pick up their students in a formalized, controlled release. The process of controlled release is called a reunification and may be necessary due to weather, a power outage, hazmat event, danger outside the school or if a crisis occurs at the school. The Standard Reunification Method is a protocol that makes this process more predictable and less chaotic for all involved.

Because a controlled release is not a typical end of school day event, a reunification may occur at a different location than the school a student attends. If this location is another school, then those students may be subject to a controlled release as well.

NOTIFICATION

Parents may be notified in a number of ways. The school or district may use its broadcast phone or text message system. In some cases, students may be asked to send a text message to their parents. A reunification text message from a student may look something like this:

"The school has closed, please pick me up at 3:25 at the main entrance. Bring your ID."

PARENT/GUARDIAN EXPECTATIONS

If a parent or guardian is notified that a controlled release and reunification is needed, there are some expectations they should be aware of. First, bring identification. That will streamline things during reunification. Second, be patient. Reunification is a process that protects the safety of the student, and provides for an accountable change of custody from the school to a recognized custodial parent or guardian.

WHAT IF A PARENT CAN'T PICK UP THEIR STUDENT?

When a parent can't immediately go to the reunification site, students will only be released to individuals previously identified as a student's emergency contact. Otherwise, the school will hold students until parents can pick up their student.

WHAT IF THE STUDENT DROVE TO SCHOOL?

There may be instances where a student is not allowed to remove a vehicle from the parking lot. In this case, parents are advised to recover the student. In some circumstances, high school students may be released on their own.

HOW IT WORKS

Students may be asked to be orderly and quiet while waiting. They may be asked to text a message to their parents or guardians, and not to message anyone else. Keeping the cellular network usage at a minimum may be important during a reunification.

REUNIFICATION CARDS

For parents, there are a couple of steps. If a parent is driving to the school, greater awareness of traffic and emergency vehicles is advised. Parents should park where indicated and not abandon vehicles. Parents are asked to go to the Reunification "Check-In" area and form lines based on the first letter of their student's last name. While in line, parents are asked to fill out a reunification card. This card is perforated and will be separated during the process. Some of the same information is repeated on both the top and bottom of the card. Parents are asked to complete all parts of the card.

In the case of multiple students being reunited, a separate card for each student needs to be completed.

BRING ID TO CHECK-IN

During check-in, identification and custody rights are confirmed. The card is separated and the bottom half is given back to the parent.

From the "Check-in" area, parents are directed to the "Reunification" area. There, a runner will take the bottom half of the card to the Student Assembly Area to recover the student or students.

Parents should be aware that, in some cases, they may be invited into the building for further information.

INTERVIEWS AND COUNSELING

In some cases, parents may be advised that a law enforcement investigation is underway and may be advised that interviews are necessary. In extreme cases, parents may be pulled aside for emergency or medical information.

© Copyright 2011-2024, All rights reserved. The "I Love U Guys" Foundation. The Standard Reunification Method and I Love U Guys are Trademarks of The "I Love U Guys" Foundation and may be registered in certain jurisdictions. This material may be duplicated for distribution by recognized schools, districts, departments and agencies. SRM Parent Handout_EN | Revised: 07/31/2024
http://iloveuguys.org